GIVE
US
THIS
SIS
DAY

Sidney Stewart

D0067999

W. W. NORTON & COMPANY

New York • *London*

Contents

GIVE US THIS DAY

1 Manila: December 1941

IN THE LAND where dead dreams go lies the city of Manila, as it was before the war. Manila, where the white man didn't work in the afternoon because it was too hot. Manila, with its beauty and its poverty and its orchids at five cents apiece.

What could a soldier do with a handful of orchids if he had no one to give them to? I used to buy those orchids. I'd pay my nickel for them and stand there awkwardly holding them in my hand. I would run my finger over the satin petals and then, embarrassed, I would give them to the first little girl I met, because there was something very lonely about buying orchids when you had no one to give them to.

Then one day I stopped thinking about orchids. The ancient Oriental city became like a frightened old woman caught in the centre of a highway crossing. People ran to and fro over the many bridges that span the dirty Pasig River flowing through the heart of Manila. It was so unlike the rivers of my native Oklahoma, where cottonwood trees line the sandy banks and clap their leaves happily in the wind.

The Pasig River swarmed with frightened life. Native

women went on beating their clothes on rocks under the lacy fronds of the palm trees, but they never took their eyes from the sky.

Eyes wide with fear, naked little boys sat on rafts of coconuts they were floating to the markets.

Turbaned Moros hurried their majestic stride among the crowds of Japanese, Chinese and Filipinos, all in their native costumes.

Only the little caramotta ponies, that gave the streets the smell of a barnyard, seemed unable to sense the vast urgency of the people. Birds still gossiped in the towering acacia trees, and blind beggars huddled against the old Spanish walls away from the feet of the crowd, crying in plaintive tones for alms.

Japanese planes circled like giant hawks searching for prey.

We crouched down in the damp dirt of a new foxhole. It was noon and the hot sun beat down from overhead. I wondered how I could keep my trousers from getting muddy, and my heavy wash-pan of a helmet flopped loosely, giving me a headache. If only it ached a little more, it might take my mind off the strange fear I had.

The fear had started three hours before, when I heard the blasting announcements about Pearl Harbor. It was a small fear then, like a cobweb that drifts across your face in a darkened room. But now I held my face against my knees, so that my friends would not see the fear written there.

The Japanese planes roared over our heads, and we snuggled closer to the ground, which smelled like a fresh-ploughed field. We are Americans, I thought, proud and sure and free. We had nothing but contempt for the stupid fools blackening the sky. The Japanese must be crazy to attack a city held by Americans.

'I'll bet this war won't last three weeks,' Rassmussen said beside me.

I wondered if it would last even one. Surely they were only making a sort of last stand. They would rather go down in glorious defeat, because to lose a war that way would be, to the Japanese, a way of saving face.

'Oh, I think it will last long enough for us to see some action, Rass.'

He smiled as I looked up. He used a characteristic gesture, pushing his straight brown hair back off his damp forehead. His kind brown eyes were serious as we heard a singing sound in the air for the first time. Did he feel deep down, as I did, that little bite of fear?

The deafening roar of explosions split the air. I bit my tongue and hid my face again. I hoped Rass wouldn't despise me if he knew I was afraid. The ground rocked beneath us, shaking as though it had life. But the explosions were a long way off. Down near the port area and along the waterfront. Yet the whining sound of the great missiles as they fell seemed close, as though they were right overhead.

We waited for more explosions but none came. Another man crawled into the foxhole and I looked around.

John Lemke panted for air. An ex-professor, John was brilliant and friendly, but most of all, orderly. His footlocker was always pointed out by the inspecting officers as an example of neatness. He removed his helmet and ran his fingers through his dark wavy hair. His clean-cut features were criss-crossed with worry.

'Say, Rass,' I laughed. 'You know what? John's got the same look on his face my Mom used to get when she figured one of my sister's cats had done something under the divan.'

'Oh well, when the all-clear sounds he'll be above it all.' Rass grinned and pushed his hair off his forehead again.

'Peons!' John did not hide his disgust. 'I just crawled over here to read my latest from home and to show you something you should have already noticed.' He pointed to new private-first-class stripes on his shirt, which was too big for him.

'Tell me, Professor,' Rass said. 'Would you say that your education had helped you to get ahead in the army?'

John nodded solemnly. 'I shall wear them as though they were a hair shirt.' Then he raised his eyes toward the sky in an attitude of holiness. 'The mighty shall be brought low,' he quoted, 'especially sergeants like you, Stew.' He looked at me and grinned.

'I give up, John. But what's so hot about this letter?'

He pulled a crumpled envelope from his side pocket and slipped out the letter. Wetting his lips, he nodded as though to a classroom of bored students.

'I quote,' he said. ' "Dear Son: I'm so glad you are in the Philippines, because I am afraid that war with Germany is inevitable. But I know that Japan will back down and you will be safe there. Safe in the Philippines throughout the war. . . ." '

We all laughed, and I could see that everyone's spirits went a little higher. Then the planes came overhead once more and we ducked down, waiting.

The bombs roared, whanging their way to the earth. The ground shook and the explosions sent the dust high into the air. There was a pungent burning smell. This time I knew the explosions were much closer. They had landed just across the river among the warehouses.

I raised my head above the foxhole. Smoke circled up beyond the old castle which was our barracks. I now had a new worry. I hated to see Estado Mayor destroyed.

The colourful old building was the ancient palace of the Spanish Mayors, who had lived here two hundred and fifty years. In those days boats had come up the Pasig River next to the castle. It was a beautiful old thing, in spite of our foxholes which guttered and criss-crossed the walled-in gardens. I looked over at the archways graced with Spanish iron lace, and the old feeling of storybook land came over me.

The mossy green walls were six to nine feet thick in some places, and most of the rooms smelled like a damp cellar. In the room that I shared with eight other men there was a mosaic map on the floor, a map of the world as it was pictured two hundred years ago, with blue stones for the water and yellow stones for the land. Many a time I had rolled over on my bunk, looking down at the map. I used to imagine a celebrated grandee standing there, with his lace collar and a long ivory pointer, pointing to the map and giving commands to the captains of his early Spanish galleons.

I was jarred out of my reverie by the moaning of the all-clear signal. It whined, gradually reaching a pitch of screaming frenzy.

We stood up, dusted ourselves off and stepped out of the foxhole. We felt like veterans who had weathered their first battle. We were a little proud of ourselves and, I know now, more than a little pathetic in our innocence. We knew so little about war.

I looked around. Some Filipino boys crouched behind the tall hibiscus bushes.

'Like the ostrich hiding his head in the sand,' Rass laughed, but when I looked at him I could see sympathy in his eyes. Then he saw I was watching him, and he brushed his hair off his forehead and looked back at our foxhole. 'I wonder what protection they think a bush would give them if a bomb lit near here,' he said.

I didn't answer, because there is a sense of protection in being hidden and I knew how the boys felt. What you cannot see does not seem so terrifying.

We walked back into our offices and went to work. New orders were out. No ties were to be worn, and no saluting was required. All of a sudden the huge lazy machine called the army was waking up and coming to life. It might even acquire some appearance of efficiency.

I was sure of it when I saw Weldon. His collar was open and the blond hair on his chest showed. He was smiling and happy, for at last he foresaw an outlet for his tremendous energy. His sleeves were rolled back, revealing his brown arms and bulging, powerful muscles.

'I wonder if they'll send us out of here to make a landing on Japan,' he said.

'Well, I don't know.' John spoke up in his grave classroom voice. 'It's highly possible. But we'll have to see how much damage they did. I was surprised that they even let those planes get over Manila.'

John looked terribly out of place in his clumsy, too-large

uniform. The private-first-class stripes on his sleeve were pitifully inadequate for a man of his background. He formed part of the incongruous picture that made up the army.

By contrast, Weldon, strong-featured and big of physique, had been a miner and had gone to work in the mines when he was only fourteen. We were all part of a group and very close friends.

Hughes came in.

'Well, what did you guys think of that one? Looks like it's really opened up for us,' he said. They all began to talk at once.

I didn't listen, because I remembered that I had been afraid. I felt inferior to them. I felt that they would hate me for it if they knew.

I looked at Hughes, with his straw hair and long nose and little moustache. Every few minutes he pulled out a benzedrine inhaler. Holding a finger over one nostril, he would press the inhaler to the other and sniff deeply. Without listening to his words, I heard his English accent. His father had brought him to America to keep him out of the war over there. We all knew the story. He had come over and when there began to be talk about the draft, he had joined the American Army. I wondered what he was thinking now.

I thought again about being afraid. I turned around and looked at Rass. He grinned, brushing his hair back nervously.

'I guess I ought to be ashamed of myself,' he said, 'but I had an awful funny feeling while I was in that foxhole.'

'I did too,' Weldon laughed. 'But that funny feeling was me being plain scared.'

I felt better, knowing they had felt the same way. Relieved, I walked over to the window. Pillars of black smoke belched high into the sky. In the distance ambulances screamed through the city, and again I felt a pang of fear. But I made up my mind to conquer it.

'What do you say we go eat?' Rass said. We turned and walked out of the building and down across the garden to Stotsenberg Hospital, where we were fed. The other boys chattered away at each other, lively as monkeys, but I didn't feel much like talking. John was silent too. As we reached the gate, I noticed a little Chinese flower girl standing there with her flowers in her hand.

She always stood there at the gate with flowers for sale. Usually we bought one and gave it to one of the girls who waited on the tables at the mess hall. But now there were tears in her eyes. Hands shaking, lips quivering, she huddled there against the wall as though the air raid was still on. Her eyes looked beyond us. I turned and behind me, down in the old walled city, I could see the smoke rising black and brown toward the sky. That was the poor section of the city. I wondered idly if she lived there.

'Come on, Sid. Let's go eat,' Weldon called.

Quickly I reached in my pocket and pulled out a dime and handed it to her. I wanted to talk to her, to help her, but there were probably many just like her all over the city. I hurried and caught up with the men.

By now ambulances were roaring around on all sides. As they sped up the streets they splashed brown gravel high into the air. They careered in front of us and across the hospital driveway.

When we reached the driveway I saw that there were

litters all over the green lawn. White sheets covered still forms, and I heard groans and cries.

I had always gotten sick at my stomach very easily. I wondered if I would get sick every time I saw someone get hurt. I can't let that happen, I thought. My friends were oddly quiet, but they walked ahead and I held back, waiting, looking at the litters stretched across the lawn.

'Hey, Stew!' I heard someone call behind me. Jackson, one of the medics I knew, was waving to me as he walked over to where I stood. His white coat was spattered with blood. He grinned, showing his white teeth.

'I just wondered if you guys knew there was a war on?' he said in his slow Texas drawl. I smiled, trying to look as unconcerned as he did.

'From the looks of things, I don't think we know it quite as much as you do.'

He laughed. 'Come over here and help me with one of these litters. Then they'll think I'm working and I can talk to you a minute.'

I wanted to say no, I've got to meet my friends. But I knew he would see through me. We walked over to one of the ambulances and started pulling out one of the litters. As it slid out of the ambulance, I reached down and grabbed the handles. We carried it to the end of the line that stretched near one of the buildings.

When we put the litter down the white sheet was trembling. The face was covered. I looked up at Jackson expectantly.

'There's nothing I can do,' he said. 'The nurses are supposed to help them first.'

I knelt down. I couldn't go off and leave without saying that someone was coming with help. Timidly I pulled back the sheet. It was a little boy. He was shaking with fright.

'What's wrong, kid? Is there anything I can do?'

He didn't say a word. But he didn't cry and I wondered if there was anything wrong at all. Then slowly he pulled his arm out from under the sheet and held it up for me to see. I felt suddenly as though someone had kicked me in the pit of the stomach.

The hand had been blown away and there was a piece of the bone sticking out. It looked dirty, and the blood was already drying. I felt sick. Jackson knelt down beside me.

'You'll be all right, kid. You'll be all right,' he said. 'One of the nurses will be here in just a minute.'

Without turning to look back, I stood up and almost ran to the mess hall. I thought I heard Jackson laughing behind me.

When I entered the mess hall, the remembered smell of mangled flesh and blood and the cooking odours from the kitchen churned around in me and I felt dizzy. Gritting my teeth, I walked over to the table and sat down with the other men. Some were teasing each other about their reactions to the things that were going on outside. I wondered if they weren't joking to cover up their true feelings.

'The report's just coming in over the radio that the Nips have bombed Clark Field and Nichols Field,' I heard one man say.

'I heard they also got Stotsenberg,' someone else threw in. I shook my head. In many parts of the islands the scene in the yard outside was being repeated. One of the waiters placed a tray before me. I didn't want to look at it. Mechanically I began to eat. As I brought the first bite to my mouth, I felt that I was going to be sick. I jumped to my feet and bolted for the door. When I reached the yard I leaned upon one of the palm trees.

I was sick, but the fresh air and the sunshine made me feel better suddenly. I leaned there, sick within myself. Would this go on every time I saw blood, every time I saw someone hurt? I felt a hand on my shoulder and I looked around. Rass was smiling.

'What's wrong, fella? Don't you feel too good?' His eyes were sympathetic. 'I went back to see if I couldn't help that little Chinese flower girl by the gate,' he said. 'What do you say we go upstairs and have a cup of coffee? Then maybe you'll feel better.'

'No, Rass, you go ahead. I want to be by myself just a little while. I'll be on up.'

He looked puzzled as though he thought I didn't want his company.

'Rass, I just want to walk around a little bit by myself and get some fresh air,' I said to reassure him. 'I feel kind of foolish about this whole thing.'

He grinned and walked on. I watched him climb the stairs, his tall form casting its shadow across the white wall. I walked over and stood by the tree and looked up into the sky. High above the greasy smoke I could see tiny white clouds and I thought, God is up there, and I began to pray.

'God, I know I haven't talked to You enough. I know I'm not always the right kind of guy . . . the kind of a guy You'd like me to be, but God, I don't ask you for very many things. I want You to help me. I can't go through this war getting sick every time I see something nasty. I'm not asking You to keep me from getting hurt or dying, because I know You've got too many men to look after. Just help me to keep from getting sick. Give me the strength to hold a man's hand when he's dying and not to be unsympathetic or hard, but still to be able to take it and go on and do the things I've got to do. Only You know what those things will be. Please help me, and thank You, God. Amen.'

Just as I finished Weldon and Hughes came out of the mess hall. Hughes was sniffing on his benzedrine inhaler as usual. Weldon came over and laid his hand on my arm.

'If anybody tries to kid you about gettin' sick, I'll knock their teeth down their throat,' he growled.

2

The bombing of the city went on day after day, and then on December 14th glaring newspaper headlines screamed that the Japanese had made landings. Eighty transports had landed at Lingayen and forty transports had landed at Lamon Bay.

The Japanese were on the island. Slowly it became clear that we were nearly helpless, that our equipment was old, and that most of our planes had been destroyed on the ground the day the war started. All we had left were five old egg-crate jobs that had been used in World War I and had been bought by the Philippine Government for training purposes. Now the radios urged the people to have faith. Help was on its way from the States.

We wondered and began to make bets on how soon it would arrive. But the planes circled above us every hour, bombing at leisure, mocking us, almost laughing at our weakness. We, the indomitable Americans, had nothing.

As the days wore on, the fires in the city filled the skies with smoke. Helplessness was written on the faces of the people in the streets. Men were rushed to the front.

Every day new lists were made up and more men left the city for the front lines. I stood one afternoon watching Weldon as he rushed about preparing his lists, lining the men up. He had tried to be fair about the men whose names he called. I stood behind him, watching him through the window. As the men lined up in the yard, somehow I felt frightened by their appearance. They didn't even know enough to wear their army shoes. They stood there wearing their oxfords as though they thought they were going to a dance. Their packs looked like fat papooses strapped to their backs.

'Fall in!' Weldon commanded. Even though I was looking at the back of his head I knew that disappointment must show on his face. He made each of them lay his pack on the ground. Weldon, who had always been so friendly, so easy to get along with, walked among them cursing and kicking their packs with his feet, watching them fall apart on the ground. Then he jerked one of the men's packs out and laid it on the ground and rolled it up quickly and neatly into a tight pack. He threw it high into the air and kicked it hard with his feet and it held together.

'I want every one of you to be able to roll a pack like that within the next five minutes. And I'm going to watch and see that you do it,' he snarled. The men began to lay them out. There was a shocked look on their faces. Here was a man, their friend, who was also a leader.

That was one of the first groups of untrained men with

old, inadequate World War I equipment to leave the city and go north. Each day there were more lists, and more men were sent. Every man knew within himself that we would be unable to hold the city of Manila. I began to fight the feeling of complete helplessness that swept over me. Oh God, if we could only hold out long enough for help to reach us from the States. Then we would not have to abandon Manila.

The streets were a humid play of hot, dusty troops. American and Filipino soldiers filled every truck that sped through the city from the south and raced north. There was a common denominator in the look of their faces, all white with coral dust, and the eyes sad and tired. One afternoon I drove one of the command cars down across the Pasig River and through the port area. Craters pitted the buildings and the roads surrounding the waterfront. The piers were tangled ribbons of steel, and the beautiful buildings were gutted and were belching black, sooty smoke. It is getting worse, I thought.

It did get worse, because each day was more hideous, and the bombings now followed nights of extreme anxiety. The wounded poured into Manila from all the outlying districts. Each morning I checked the casualty lists for news of my friends, but none of their names matched those on the lists. Enemy planes had successfully cleared the air of our few decrepit aeroplanes. Now they circled low over the city, hour after hour, either leisurely observing or bombing at will.

Thousands of Japanese troops were being landed at our most vulnerable points on Luzon. They were pushing with great speed down the great central valley that ran the length of the island, thrusting vast finger-like prongs toward the city of Manila. Gloom and apprehension hung over the city. Manila was doomed. Already the streets were ghost-like. All available cars and buses had been commandeered by the quickly mobilized Philippine Army. Families fleeing toward the provinces clogged the roads, for at least in the country there would be food if they were besieged.

Christmas Eve we worked all night preparing the orders and dividing the men into groups that would be the last troops to leave the city, if it became necessary. The 'phones rang incessantly, giving the latest orders and the news of the Japanese onslaught. I watched the lieutenant lift the 'phone, and his sleepless eyes became suddenly grave.

'This must be nearly it,' he said, replacing the receiver. 'Manila has been declared an open city.' His face looked old and tired and very sad. 'They're not going to fight for it.'

'My God!' I exploded. 'What about the thousands of wounded here in the city? What are we gonna do? Are they just going off and leaving them here? And what about the medics here with them? Just leave them to face these yellow bastards and get their throats cut?'

'Stewart,' the lieutenant said grimly. 'You and I just happen to be about the lowest level in this army. It's not our business to worry about it.'

'Americans running out!' Weldon spat contemptuously in his wastebasket. 'Who ever heard of such a thing?'

I walked over and looked out through the darkened window. I bit my tongue to hold back the tears. Across the city I could hear the faint music and the sound of voices singing, 'Silent Night, Holy Night'. Then the telephone jarred the air with an insistent ringing. I did not listen to the conversation which droned like a monologue through the smoke-filled room. Cigarette stubs, ashes and crumpled wads of paper littered the floor. On the desk were dirty coffee cups and spilled sugar. Weldon slumped over his desk, his face buried in his arms. Part of the telephone conversation jerked me back to reality.

'Start moving part of the men out of the city by noon today, groups of fifty, you say?' The clerk repeated the orders monotonously. Weldon sat up in his chair and yawned, stretching his arms like a huge cat.

'I've got some news I haven't told you,' he said. 'We're going to be the last troops to leave the city.'

'I wish we didn't have to leave at all, Weldon.' I turned to the door. 'I'm going to walk out and see if I can't get a little air.'

I made my way across the yard toward the empty streets, trying to forget that this was Christmas Eve and that soon it would be Christmas morning, 1941. The faint light of the tropical dawn was already giving the horizon a rosy glow. I reached the ruins of the ancient Santo Domingo Church, wondering if the gifts I had sent home would be there for them to open this morning. Looking across the rubble and the ashes, I watched the Filipinos kneeling.

Above them the black rafters stretched like the ribs of a skeleton. Along the half-destroyed walls still clung the relics and images that mean so much to the Filipino Catholics. On the high wall above the altar I noticed the unscarred figure of Christ, whose sad face looked down upon the ruins and the people gathered to honour his birth. Up the street floated the soft music of voices singing, 'Joy to the World, The Lord Has Come'.

Tears clouded my eyes and suddenly I felt lonely and homesick.

The day after Christmas, just as darkness was beginning to settle over the city, Rassmussen and I drove through the streets in search of a food market. We felt sure that something resembling fresh vegetables could be found, but everywhere we turned there were only empty stalls.

The vacant loneliness of the city made me sad. I missed the hurried scenes of the past few days, when trucks had sped through the city loaded with weary soldiers. There had been no laughter in them, just truck after truck, filled with men, covered with dust from the coral roads. The masks of dust were like shrouds covering them from head to toe. Only their eyes were alive, dark sad eyes that burned into your soul so that you saw them long after the trucks had gone. The air reverberated with a recurring roar as demolition squads laid waste everything in the city that might be used by the oncoming enemy. There were no patterns to the explosions, and I would catch myself listening to their irregular booming, blasting, booming.

Burning oil tanks sent forth pitch-black clouds. They wove themselves into a dirty black cloth that settled back over the city, giving it an appearance of a weeping widow. We turned down street after street that stretched away grey and empty, deserted, and strangely sad. A desperate feeling of helplessness gripped me. I kept silent.

I could not see Rassmussen's eyes, but the lines about his jaw were tight with feeling. He brushed the hair off his forehead nervously. On the doors of many of the grey little houses were signs in school chalk, written in English and Japanese, 'This is only a poor Filipino home'. The white signs seemed to burn with a feeling of surrender and an appeal for mercy from the conquering enemy.

'Can't say as I blame them much,' Rass said huskily. 'Maybe the Nips will treat the natives okay.'

'We can't tell yet, Rass.' I could not help thinking of the brutal sack of Nanking. Stories of the atrocities committed throughout China by the Japanese were common talk in Manila. I doubted if there was much hope there.

I turned the heavy command car down another street. Our chances of finding fresh vegetables were slim. Shopkeepers shook their heads sadly. They stood in their doorways and gazed with hopeless bewilderment as each new column of smoke gushed into the air. We gave up at last and I turned the car back toward headquarters.

Occasionally we passed small groups of Filipinos who looked at us with amazement. To the Filipino the situation was incomprehensible. We had always been the dominant, unconquerable Americans, almost like gods. But now we were running and leaving them to their fate. A fate that seemed to hold little chance of being better than the rape and the horror of China. Even the dirty little urchins no longer yelled to us or held up their grimy fingers to form a 'V' for victory. We had become a part of the melancholia of the doomed and burning city.

'Stewart, let's drive by the Manila Hotel,' Rass said suddenly. 'I'll bet we could get a drink there.'

'Why, Rass, we haven't got any dough. Besides we look like the wrath of God.'

'Aw, Stewart, you always have to be a prima donna. They know there's a war going on. I bet they'd be glad to give us a drink,' and he grinned. 'Besides,' he said, 'aren't we going to make the world safe for democracy, or something?'

'Yeh, but I bet those poor people out there are wishing we'd make the city safe for them.' I turned the car across the bridge and down Dewey Boulevard and toward the world-famous hotel.

'Every time I see a civilian American I feel sorry for them. They don't know what to expect. They don't know whether the Nips will bayonet them right in the guts and then rape their wives, or what.' Suddenly I wanted to change the subject. 'Oh well, I'm glad to try and bum a drink.'

Heading the car up the long curving driveway toward the impressive entrance of the hotel, I began to feel a little foolish. Neither one of us had been able to afford to go to this luxurious centre for world travellers before.

I brought the car to a stop right in front and we both jumped to the ground. Still at the entrance, the impeccable, uniformed doorman smiled, and I knew that to him we both looked like tramps. He bowed and opened the door with the same flourish he had formerly given to celebrated guests. We stepped into the brilliantly lighted lobby.

It was crowded, and attendants moved among the guests with silent efficiency. The women wore beautiful gowns and most of the men were dressed in evening suits. I was sorry we had come.

The place rang with laughter and lighthearted music floated from the dance floor. I could not help feeling that the laughter was false and that these people were trying desperately to forget the war-torn city which lay beyond the tall blue glass windows. Many were dancing, but the floor was not crowded and we cut across it toward the bar.

Like a bad dream we carried with us the look of the strife beyond the walls and the burning city.

One couple turned and faced us. The man was tall and handsome and had black wavy hair. He was dressed in a white evening jacket and held a gold cigarette lighter in his outstretched hand. The flame of the lighter threw an orange halo over the girl's face as she leaned forward to light her cigarette. I could see that her hand trembled, but she straightened and blew a smoke ring that floated and broke in the faint breeze. Her brittle laugh seemed to catch in the air.

'I wired Mom that it would be just a fabulous adventure. Fabulous.'

She laughed again and tossed her auburn hair so that it caught the mirrored lights from the ceiling. A dragon of green sequins sparkled down her black skirt. She looked at us, and shuddered.

As we crossed the floor the other guests looked at us also and fell silent. The music was suddenly flat. I would gladly have turned and ducked out of the place. If only Rass would suggest it.

'Joe, how about a drink?' Rass asked, as we slid onto the rotating bar stools. 'We haven't any money though,' he added. 'Uncle Sam has been too busy to pay us lately.'

The bartender smiled and wiped an imaginary spot on the chromium-topped counter.

'Anything you wish is on us,' he said.

'Yep, you can just about have the house,' a nervous blonde chirped on the stool next to me. 'You fellows aren't planning on staying for the reception, I hope?'

'What reception?' I asked without thinking.

'Oh, don't act naïve,' she said bitterly, stamping her cigarette deliberately on the polished bar. 'We know what's going on. Why do you think everyone around here is acting so gigglesome?' She pointed her thumb back over her bare shoulder. 'We know where we're headed in a few days. Won't I look pretty behind barbed wire?' She shrugged her shoulders. 'I hope those yellow slant eyes will like this dress.'

She was exquisitely dressed in yellow satin. The strapless evening gown fitted tightly across her waist, accentuating the breadth of her figure, and the gold sequins on her dress sparkled quickly with each rise and fall of her bosom in breathing. I let my eyes travel from the small opening of her breasts upward, noticing the sensitive lips and the aristocratic brow for the first time. Her golden hair was held in place by a jewelled clip, but it fell and swayed lazily across her bare shoulders. I had not realized how intensely I stared until she smiled.

'You want to dance?' she said. 'I'd hate to be attacked right here at the bar. How long has it been since you've talked to an American girl, anyway?'

'Well—' Noticing the well-dressed Europeans and Americans in their white evening jackets, I hesitated.

'Come on, don't be silly,' she said. 'I probably would never have spoken to you if you were dressed in white tie and tails. You look better to me than any of those frightened fools anyway.'

It was like a dream, floating across the floor with her in my arms, and her faint perfume was so exciting that unconsciously I tightened my grip at the small of her back. I choked down the desire to bite her right on the pink flesh at the nape of her neck.

'I haven't danced with a white—I mean, an American girl since I left the States,' I stuttered.

She laughed. 'You nearly slipped then. Oh, we've been around. The international set I think they call us. Probably the spoiled Miss Rich-Bitches to you, though.' There was a challenge in her eyes and I smiled. The music stopped and I realized we were practically the only ones on the floor.

'Let's go out on the balcony and look at the Bay,' she suggested. 'Who knows there might even be a moon. Not that you seem to need one.'

She led the way through the potted palms and out across the stone terrace.

We walked to the low wall and stood for a moment looking out across the bay. A few ships still burned and an occasional explosion sent sparks dancing high into the sky. There was no moon but it was clear weather. The white tops of the waves raced each other to the shore.

'In some ways these night fires are really beautiful.' She sighed and leaned back against my arm. 'You usually expect so much noise with fires, fire engines and all. But these fires seem to be just the flowing aftermath of something. They just go on sending up their smoke.'

She sat down on the sea wall, leaving room for me beside her. I stood for a little while, fascinated by the bronze gleam the ship fires gave her hair, until she grasped my hand and pulled me down beside her.

'You would notice, if you'd take your eyes off me long enough, that Cavite Navy Station, burning out there across the bay, looks like an early morning sunrise.' Her voice was low and lovely.

'My name is Janet,' she said, trying to catch her breath. 'Not that it makes any difference.'

I wanted to say, 'Relax, kid, don't try to laugh it off. Go ahead, cry if you want to'. But I couldn't speak, for somehow I knew she was braver than I was. She didn't know what was coming tomorrow or the next day or the next.

The fires burned day after day. Explosions no longer shook the city, but black smoke and streaks of flame from the burning oil tanks gave each night an end-of-the-world appearance. Estado Mayor was now merely an empty palace, echoing hollowly the sounds made by the few men left behind. Manila had been declared open to the world and undefended, in the hope of sparing the city wanton destruction. With the soldiers gone, and trucks and automobiles commandeered by the retreating army, the civilians were helpless beneath the ominous roar of the Japanese planes circling above the city.

The wounded, blasted by the daily bombings, died in the streets where they lay. The stench from the rotting bodies was beginning to permeate the air. Word came finally that the last group of soldiers would leave tonight on a boat for Corregidor and then Bataan.

I began to wonder what our chances were for making it. Slim perhaps, but then we would have the cover of the night.

The day seemed long but in the afternoon I walked out into the garden, just walking, for most of our work was done.

'Hello, Sid!'

Surprised, I turned around. Mrs Harding was standing

near the gate, holding her small daughter by the hand. I smiled and walked toward her. There were deep lines of worry in her face and her eyes seemed tired and sad. Her soft brown hair, usually so well kept, was mussed as though by the wind. She had been like a mother to all of us. The wife of an English missionary in the Islands, she had kept her home open to us. I began to ache inside, realizing now what she faced.

'Sid,' she said. 'I thought you had gone many days ago with the rest. If I had known you were still here I would have come and talked to you. You see, my husband was cut off at Baguio by the Japanese, and he wasn't able to make it back to Manila—,' she choked and then continued. 'I'm trying awfully hard. I would not be afraid for myself, if only it were not for the child.' Then she began to cry. 'Oh, why must the Americans run off and leave the city like this? There's no one here to advise us what to do. And no one to protect us.'

I bit my lip. I felt small and helpless. 'Don't blame us. Don't blame the Americans,' I said desperately. 'We're not running out because we want to.' I began to finger in my pockets. I had a ten-centavo piece, the only money I had. I didn't know where I could get any more.

'The only advice I can give you is, get whatever money you can and hold on to it. Buy what supplies you need for at least two weeks and then lock yourself in your house and stay there.' I tried to make my voice sound free and hopeful, but I wasn't. She had always tried to make us feel at home and less lonesome in the Islands. I bent down and picked up a sandstone from the gravelled walk. The soldiers had

told her all their troubles. She was such a little woman, it
seemed to me now, standing with the child twisting and
pulling at the skirt of her dress.

'Sid—I lost so many friends in the sacking of Nanking.'
Her voice was hollow and her lip trembled. 'I wonder if
they will commit the same atrocities here?'

'Oh, God!' I exploded, but her face held the look I had
seen once on a man who had run over his own child. 'Don't
let yourself even think about such things. Do you have any
servants that are faithful and that will stand by you?'

'Yes, I have two, Mary and Romulo. But they couldn't
do anything.' Tears glistened on her cheeks and she reached
down and patted her little girl's golden hair.

'Well now, listen to me.' I tossed the sandstone against
a palm tree. 'When you go home, stay there and don't go
out for anything. If you need anything, send out one of
your servants. You see, the first troops entering the city will
be undisciplined soldiers, but then in a couple of days the
Japanese officers will move in. They'll protect you. They
won't treat you like a Chinese. You're a white woman and
the Japanese will realize that here.' I ran my hand across
my forehead and it was wet. I realized how desperately I
was trying to give her some hope.

'The Americans will retake Manila within a month at
least,' I said confidently. 'It takes a long time for help to
get here from the States, and we know that it's already on
the way.'

'Sid,' she said tenderly. 'You pray, don't you?'

I looked down at the ground. 'Sure, sure, lots of times.'
She smiled when I looked up, then ran her hand over

her light brown hair, patting it in place. She reached down and took the child's hand and straightened her skirt.

'Well, goodbye, Sid.' She held out her hand and her chin was higher and more determined. 'And please—let's pray for each other.'

She turned and walked slowly up the deserted street. The child holding her hand skipped and hopped with gay abandon, stopping every so often to point at things along the way. I watched them until they disappeared, but the helplessness and fear I felt for her made me sick inside. I didn't really believe that stuff about the Japanese treating her better than they had the Chinese. Suddenly I wanted to curse and smash my fist into something—something to break the feeling of helplessness.

3

It was definite. We would leave at twelve midnight. The last of the inter-island steamers was lying in readiness down at the port area. The men had worked in the afternoon to get an old truck ready to take us through the streets of the city. Now most of them were resting.

I sat alone in the office, staring at the heavy blackout curtains over the big archway. The electricity had been off for hours and the only light was from three large candles. As they burned down they flickered and made strange shadows across the littered office. I wondered how it would be, what things were like in Bataan, how many hours it would take us to get there.

Suddenly I felt a presence in the room. I turned and looked up. It was a rather small man, dressed in the white tropical habit of a priest. He didn't say a word, but in his

sad eyes I felt a strength. I looked at him standing there in
the arched doorway of the old castle for a moment. His
kind, thin face was tanned and softly crossed with lines
that indicated a quickness to smile or to deepen with sympathy. His sparse sandy hair was partially grey. It seemed
natural for him to be there. I looked at his face again and
he was smiling. I thought he had the kindest smile I had
ever seen.

'I'm a Catholic priest, son.' His voice was soothing. 'I
heard you boys were leaving in an hour or so. I wondered
if there were any of you who would like to talk to a priest,
someone who might want to go to confession?'

I stood up and motioned for him to sit down in one of
the chairs. We had one comfortable chair, a big leather-
covered seat. He looked small and insignificant in it, and
yet a sense of great strength emanated from him.

'Well, Father, I'm not a Catholic,' I said. My mind began
to race over the list of the men who were still there, checking them off. I knew that none of them was Catholic.

'That's all right, son,' he said. 'Even though there are no
Catholics, maybe some boy would like to talk to me. I could
help that way.'

I smiled. There was an odd bond of understanding between us.

'I've been a teacher here in Manila for many years now.'
His voice was clear and soft. 'I had a little school of my
own. I used to have many little Filipino children, but'—he
looked lonely—'my school isn't here any more.' He turned
his face away as if he were examining the blackout curtains.
The lines of the candle made his head seem small, and his
hair was thinning. He turned again.

'It burned yesterday and the school isn't any more,' he said flatly. I had the feeling that I was watching a man whose life's work had been destroyed. Yet there was not a trace of sadness in his voice. It was as though that had passed, and that was the way things were. We talked for a while. I told him about my home in the States. We talked about going to Bataan. About help that would be coming from the States. When I looked up again I saw a new light in his eyes.

'I wonder if there are enough priests in Bataan. They don't need me here in Manila. There are many priests for the people here in the city.' There was hope in his voice. 'I wonder if I could go with you to Bataan. I'm sure that they need me there.'

I looked at him, studying the long, flowing, white tropical habit. It would be out of place there in the jungle. He smiled as he caught what I was thinking.

'I would have to wear other clothes, of course. Here in the Islands, we always wear our habits. The Filipinos would not know we were priests if we did not dress as priests.' I nodded just as Lieutenant Lunnie came into the room, glancing at his wrist watch.

'We have only twenty minutes now,' he said. As I stood up I realized I did not know the priest's name. But he smiled and reached out his hand.

'I'm Father Cummings,' he said. 'Father Bill Cummings.' After they shook hands he reached over and shook my hand.

'Lieutenant Lunnie—uh—Father Cummings would like to go with us to Bataan,' I said.

'Why, we're not authorized to take anyone else.' Lunnie looked dismayed. 'I have no authorization for such a thing.'

'Lieutenant, do you know how many men are going at all?' I asked pointedly.

'Well, no, I'm not sure. I'm sure there will be some men from the other sections of the city but—.'

'Well, Lieutenant, the authorization does not list any exact number, and the man wants to go.' I spoke with conviction. 'He feels that there will be men there who will need him.'

The lieutenant turned and the eyes of the two men met. They looked at each other for a moment without speaking. Lunnie nodded his head and turned to me.

'Well, have him ready with the men when the whistle blows. The truck will be right outside. We're going to have some trouble getting through the streets. They're covered with debris. It will take time to get there, so we're going to leave exactly on time.' With a nod he left us alone to wait.

When the whistle blew the men crowded out of the building. I blew out the candles one by one. Before I blew out the last candle I looked around the office. I hated to leave it. I loved the old castle. It was a part of the romance and colour of the Islands. A castle many years older than I was, that probably would stand long after I was gone.

After climbing up into the back of the truck I reached down for Father Cummings' hand and pulled him up. Weldon helped Hughes first and then climbed in himself. Rass and John swung themselves in without speaking. I introduced them to the priest in low tones. There was no reason for whispering, but the blackness of the night and the slow, apprehensive movement of the truck down the gravelled drive gave us a feeling of secrecy and conspiracy. The truck moved without lights, groaning along in low gear while we searched the sky for enemy planes. We stopped occasionally, the men taking turns to jump down and move pieces of debris or a fallen tree out of the road.

Nearly an hour went by before we reached the port area. The truck shuddered to silence. In the inky blackness we made our way by putting our hands on the men in front of us. We stumbled up the gangplank with our packs on. Our 1918 messkits and canteens were clanging at our sides. Father Cummings' white tropical habit stood out sharp and somehow comforting against the darkness.

Once on the deck of the ship, which smelled like rancid butter from its former cargoes of coconut oil, I could see the faces of the crew in the faint light. Their eyes told me how anxious they were for us to be loaded and the boat cut away from the pier. The kept looking up at the sky. Hughes sniffed at his inhaler, and Rass nervously brushed his hair off his forehead. As soon as we were all loaded the ship pulled silently away from the pier. The short strip of water grew wider and wider between us and shore.

Father Cummings and I leaned against the rail watching. The strip of water grew wider. At last we had a full view of the burning city. The flames licked against the night and sparks cast themselves high into the sky and fell back like Roman candles. Without looking at him I knew how he must feel. Much of his life lay behind him there in the city. Yet he was leaving for the greater dangers of Bataan to bring help to soldiers he felt needed him.

'They don't need me any more, there in the city. I hope the boys out there will want my help.'

I reached over and gripped his hand.

'They'll need you, Father. Where we're going, we'll all need you.'

The smile of gratitude on his face made me feel much better. Then I noticed his tropical habit again.

'But, Father,' I said, 'you won't be able to wear those clothes. Not where we're going.'

'Well, surely when we get there, someone will give me something to wear.'

I always had more stuff than I needed. 'I think I've got something you can wear,' I said. I reached behind me and slipped off my pack, pulling out a shirt and a pair of trousers and a belt.

'Here, try these on.'

He slid out of his white habit. When he put on my shirt I realized for the first time how small he was. There was such a feeling of strength in the man that he had seemed to me much larger.

'They're a little big, aren't they?' he laughed. The shoulder line of the shirt fell low on his arms and the sleeves dangled over his hands. We rolled the sleeves back up over his hands and turned the length of the trousers up. He tightened the belt, lapping it over.

'You must be nearly six feet four, aren't you?' he asked.

'Almost, Father,' I said. 'But somehow I don't feel as big as you.' He laughed and gripped my hand.

All night we sat together on the boat watching the distance to the shore grow farther away. Now there was only a faint glow of the fires 'way in the distance, and the sun was coming up. Suddenly I heard the roar of planes in the air. I could see the deadly little forms high against the morning blue. There was fear on the faces of the men around me and I was scared too, for we had nowhere to hide. We had no protection. Then I felt someone put his hand on my arm.

'Don't be afraid, son. Don't be afraid.' I turned and looked into Father Cummings' eyes. They were calm and he smiled. 'You know, son, the two strongest forces in mankind, the two strongest forces on earth, are fear and love. You might call love, faith. The two forces cannot exist side by side. If you have enough faith, you will have no fear.'

If only I had enough faith, I thought. But I looked up into the sky again, watching those deadly little shapes, like silver gnats high in the burning tropical dawn. When I looked back into his face my fear suddenly disappeared. I knew that if he wasn't afraid, then I wasn't going to be. I wasn't going to let him see my fear. Suddenly the planes disappeared and barges were brought along the side of the ship.

A small portable gangplank was laid down to one of the barges. We grabbed up our gear and began working our way off the ship. My friends and I stuck together closely. We felt strong as long as we stayed together. When we reached the barge, a little motor boat began to tug it out toward the shore.

'Father Cummings,' Rass asked the priest, 'what is this little place we're pulling into, do you know?'

'This is Lamay, son. It's a little native *barrio* on the bay side of Bataan.'

When the barge reached the shore we unloaded. We walked up to the dusty road and waited. Finally orders came and we were assigned. We were going to march north into battle.

'I have to leave you here,' Father Cummings said, giving me his hand. 'We will see each other again, I feel it,' he said. 'I have to go back to report to someone who is head

of the Chaplains' Corps. He will assign me somewhere. I
wish that it could be with you boys, but I'll go wherever he
tells me. Remember to think of God, wherever you go, and
it will be easier for you, whatever comes.'

We marched off up the road.

'I can't forget the feeling of strength that man conveyed
to us,' Rass said. 'That sense of inner peace that had strength
within it.'

We walked on. None of us was sure what our fate would
be. We talked about the help that was coming soon from
the States.

2 Bataan Peninsula, Luzon, Philippine Islands: January 1942

FLASHES of artillery fire splashed the early evening sky with lightning. The rumbling thunder of the explosions gave an ominous foretaste of the terror to come. The jungle night pressed down like a black oiled tarpaulin. Huge trees stood stripped, holding up their naked branches, pleading to the war god, while bullets ricocheted and sang through the air. Grey smoke, pungent and biting, mingled with the silky dust floating up from the jungle floor and clinging like dense smog to the tops of the broken trees. Birds and monkeys screamed with fear and glared at the tired soldiers who rested beneath the trees.

'It's going to be the bloody devil, moving forward in the morning,' Hughes groaned in his well-defined English accent. Mechanically he searched his pockets for his nose inhaler. 'I don't really see why in hell we have to move up.'

'Well,' Weldon answered in the patient, fatherly voice he always used with Hughes, 'we've got to hold this line so it means we've got to move forward at least half a mile to be in line with the Fifty-first.' His dirty shirt clung to his back damp with sweat, showing the powerful outline of his muscles as he wiped his tired face. Removing his helmet, he

42

began swinging it by the chin strap. 'And that's gonna be rough.'

The sun was sinking fast, resting now on the green crest of the Marivales Mountains. After the rainy season is gone in the jungles of Bataan for a few months the graded hues of brilliant green sparkle like emeralds in the hot sun which sifts through the giant acacia leaves. The waxy elephant-ear leaves of the gobi plant hide secretive golden orchids. Wild climbing bougainvillea runs through the trees like red fire, and the earth is rich and slippery like black potter's clay.

But as the months go by without rain, the ground becomes hard and breaks in spider-web cracks like cold lava. Then in the two months before the rains come again, toward the last of April, all moisture is gone and the jungle floor is ankle-deep in fine silt, like old attic dust settled for centuries.

The five of us sat on the edge of our narrow trench foxhole, our feet resting inside it. The silky white dust made a common denominator of our faces, and only the oily sweat outlining in brown dirt the nose, eyes and mouth made a difference.

Rass's face was impassive under the dust. But I could not help smiling as I watched his severe, determined jaw, which always looked as though life were giving him an argument he would not accept. Because he seldom cursed and would listen for hours while men told him their troubles, the men in the company had begun to call him, affectionately, 'the preacher.'

Twice he turned red in the face and wanted to fight when a man called him that, but the others had laughed him out of it. But to me, his closest friend, he was given to moods as variable as the wind. When he was most afraid, he risked his life to help someone else. He said to me he did it to prove to himself that he wasn't a coward, in spite of the fear that clawed at his stomach.

A shell tore through the sky with the sound of wind ripping a canvas tent. Rass's honest brown eyes grew serious. His hand went up in his habitual gesture, pushing back the loose hair that fell across his forehead.

John coughed, quickly covering his mouth with his small hand. He coughed too much lately, always blaming it on the infernal dust. No one knew how much he dreamed of being back in a classroom. The clean, fragile cut of his features stood out beneath the dust. His wavy brown hair was almost white with the fine silt. Unlike the rest of us, he seldom complained about the life we lived, but held up under it with a kind of passive resistance. When he talked of home, his eyes would brighten, and I could almost see the lakes of Wisconsin reflected there.

It was restful sitting still, but my feet hurt. It seemed like years since I had had my shoes off. Hughes had found his inhaler and I wondered if its constant use was not somehow responsible for the length of his nose. His clear blue eyes peered through the dust mask, anxiously searching the sky, ready to be the first to dive for the foxhole.

We could hear the shelling up on the hillside and the crashing and whining as the shells went through the air. But at least we were having a break. There was only an occasional zinging of snipers' bullets whizzing and biting at the leaves of the trees. Suddenly a shell shattered alarmingly close over our heads. We ducked down into the trench again and then stood up when no more came. Just a momentary fright. I couldn't help comparing that fright to the greater, overall fear.

Fright is a thing of the moment, attacking as a cornered animal does, on a second's notice. But fear is an ulcerous growth, pulsating and alive, attached to you like a jungle leech. No fire under the exploding heavens can burn it free. Sometimes it is not so bad, but then again it grips you and binds you as though it will not allow you the smallest movement. Again, at other times, through absolute weariness, you feel you can be free from it. But no, you can only hope to control it. It is always there. It lives with you, whispering sounds easily heard above the crashing world around you, and you are two people, yourself, and the fear that lives within you. When a man is blown to pieces beside you, it hammers in your brain and makes you smell the warm, sickening blood, a smell which even the acrid powder smoke cannot drive away. Oh dear God, give us rest. Not rest from weariness, for gladly we would never close our eyes if only that gnawing fear would die.

Once a huge shell struck the top of a tree without exploding. The shell bounced to the ground and waddled down the incline toward our foxhole, moving like a galvanized washtub rolling on its side. Afraid to breathe, we watched it waddle towards us. It reached the edge of the foxhole and rolled in, snuggling against us, warm and alive. When it didn't go off, I laughed with hysterical uncontrolled relief. Then, realizing, I caught my breath hard.

Farno, the Italian boy in the trench with me, had been destroyed by a force greater than the explosive. His mind was gone and he lay there whimpering, absolutely paralysed, unable even to talk. Finally he died, his pleading eyes mirroring like cold glass the reflection of the white bursts of smoke in the blue tropical sky. Yes, the greatest devil is fear.

'I used to think I knew what fear was,' Weldon said. 'When I was a kid I used to go down in the mines. The cold, damp darkness was so black you couldn't see your hand. But it wasn't like this. It didn't eat on you.'

We had been together so long and through so much that sometimes it wasn't necessary to talk. Often I thought about something and without explanation one of my friends would begin discussing the same subject, penetrating the thought at the level I had just reached.

When the night came the darkness of the jungle was a sinister thing, with strange gleams of artillery fire and the bursting of shells, or a whining, shuddering noise as they rose overhead. One night we heard someone crying. The lost weeping of a man who is hurt and alone. It stopped, started, stopped. We tried to ignore it, for the shelling was close now. But the crying went on very near to us. Rass, beside me, grew more tense and nervous with each sob.

'Whoever that guy is, he's not very far from us,' he said hoarsely. 'I can't stand lying here. We won't be able to sleep with him crying all night. I've got to go see if I can't help him.'

'Aw, you better take it easy, Rass,' I said. 'Better stay where you are. You're better off right here now where y'are.' I couldn't see his face in the dark, but I sensed his impatience.

'Nope, I think I can get him.' He was on his knees and crawling out of the foxhole. I raised my head and watched him. The shells began exploding faster around us. Mortar blast, but they were deadly. Then a machine gun opened up, sending small streaks of light, red tracers. I could hear them like bees brushing through the foliage of the trees. A giant flare burst. In the ghostly day of the magnesium I could see that Rass had reached the wounded man, not over twenty-five feet away. He began working with him.

'Hey, Stew!' I heard him call. 'You're gonna have to help me with this guy. It'll take two of us to get him over there.'

'Oh, hell,' I thought as the flare went out. 'Rass has always got to be doin' something like this.' I crawled out, hugging the earth. Almost digging a groove with my chin, snaking my way across the ground until I reached them. In the faint flickering of the explosions he looked to be an awfully small man. I grabbed him by the shoulders. Rass was working on one side, but we had to raise ourselves to our knees to start moving him back. We started pulling him and I heard him grit his teeth. Then he cried out in pain.

'You'll have to take this till we can get you over here,' Rass said. We moved him slowly until we got him back down into the foxhole. Rass bent down over him, examining him, and I opened up my medical aid kit. He was just a young kid. Rass opened his shirt, and in the light of another flare I looked down. It was no use, no use at all. The kid had taken a large piece of shell right in the pit of his stomach. He was ripped open and part of his insides was gone.

'I'll have to wait until daylight before I can do anything for you, kid,' Rass said. 'It won't be long now. I'll try to get you to a doctor when it gets light.'

I could hear the even snoring of Hughes and the deep steady breathing of John. They were sound asleep. But Weldon was restless. We waited beside the boy for another light. When it came I could see how young he was. So very young. He didn't seem old enough to be a soldier.

'I'm afraid to die,' he pleaded. 'I'm so scared of dying and I feel kinda cold. My legs feel cold.' He began to weep again. 'I'm so afraid to die.' Rass patted him on the arm, and he looked up with bright, childlike eyes. 'I don't hurt much, but I'm scared t'die. I dunno what's gonna happen to me after I'm dead. I dunno where I'm goin'.'

'Why, kid,' Rass said softly. 'Don't you know anything about God? Don't you know anything about Heaven?'

'I don't know nothin' about dyin',' the kid said, staring with his wide, frightened eyes. 'I don't know about God. I've never been to church in my life.' I looked at Rass's face and I could see the puzzled, incredulous stare there. The kid must have noticed it too, because he spoke again.

'You see, I never did have a Dad, that is if I did, I never did know it. Nobody but just me and my Mom, and she worked all the time. When I was old enough, I got a job. I just never did go to church.' He began to cry again as a flare went out. 'I'm so afraid to die.' Then he went on. 'I got permission from my Mom to join the army. I wasn't old enough.'

Rass reached over and caught hold of his hand.

'Now, kid, listen to me,' Rass said firmly. 'Don't think about dying. Just listen to what I have to tell you.' I wondered what he was going to say. The other men were beginning to stir and pretty soon the call would come and we'd have to move forward. The shells were opening up thick now. The firing of the machine guns sent a ripping whirr above us. I found myself listening to Rass as he talked to the boy, watching his sensitive face as he formed each word with great conviction.

'You know, kid, God made this earth we live on. He made these trees, He made everything, and He made man. God put that part in every man that is good. So a man would know the difference when he was doing the right thing and when he wasn't. I guess you know just like I do that some men fail that little part of God inside of themselves. Some men, a lot of us, are just ornery enough to destroy it.

'There was a time, a long time ago, when most of the men on this earth didn't pay much attention to God. Lots of them didn't pay any attention, and so God had a Son of his own. He let Him be born, right here on earth, so He could show men the right way. Show them that as long as they believed in Him and had faith they'd find out that this life here, this was just sort of a preliminary. If we came through this test the right way, we would have a life forever, a good life with no shells or pain or sorrow, a life when things were like you dream. He promised it, kid. He said, "If you believe in Me, and believe in My Son, ye shall have life everlasting." He said that in the Bible, and the Bible is God's book.' Rass took his helmet off and pushed his hair back as his eyes searched the early morning sky, now turning a dark green in the east.

'You ever walked along and seen flowers blooming, and the buds coming out on the trees? You didn't have anything to do with those, did you? But there they are. Something made those possible, and Something never forgets. Every spring, there they are. That's God, kid, and he won't forget you either. If you just believe, you'll go where people are never tired, or scared, or hurt. It's all that simple. If you believe in God and believe in His Son, why, you haven't got anything to be afraid of. Dying means you've just passed a test.'

I could just see the kid's face now. He never took his eyes from Rass's face, and they had the look of a child. His face was bloodless white and his lips trembled as he lay quiet. I heard Weldon cough and sit up, but I didn't look at him for fear the soft glow of dawn would reveal how deeply I was moved.

Rass cleared his throat and went on. 'It's like winning a medal—like going home.'

Tears kept forming in my eyes as I listened to him. I knew Rass was a little sheepish about talking that way in front of the rest of us. But we had all known that Rass, with his staunch church background, was more apt to show his religion than the rest of us. I looked at the kid and there was a smile on his face. He was smiling up at Rass as though Rass had shown him something no one else ever had.

'I'm not afraid no more,' he said. 'I'm not afraid now.' He closed his eyes. Then his head fell over to the side, and suddenly I heard someone yell.

'Hey, you guys, we gotta get movin'. We gotta get goin'.'

Mechanically we began to adjust our helmets.

'If anybody kids Rass for talking like that I'll knock their teeth down their throat,' Weldon said huskily. None of us answered or looked at each other.

Gritting my teeth, I tried not to think of what we had to do. Half a mile to go forward and the Japs would contest every foot. We fixed our guns and waited for the order.

'All right! On your feet, men! Let's go!'

We jumped up and began running across the broken ground. Shells came bursting and I saw a man fall. The bullets were making their thin, nasty little noises and there was a horrible crashing around me. Then I heard a plane diving overhead. Ahead of me I could see a large bomb crater. I sprinted for it just as I heard the whine of the bombs coming toward the earth. I dived for it. Just as I hit the bottom of the crater I felt another man jump in beside me.

'Phew,' I said fervently. 'We made that just in time!' I turned and with a shock clear through I saw he was a Japanese. Automatically, before he could raise his rifle, I jerked out my forty-five. It was an ancient Colt single-action, the kind the Army had used 'way back in Indian fighting days, but it was all they'd had to give me. Before he'd more than twitched I had him covered.

'Awright, bud! You're mine.' I gulped, my voice high and unreal. He looked at me strangely. He knew it was useless to lift his rifle. Slowly he laid it in front of him on the ground. I motioned with my hand for him to push it over. He kicked it with his foot. We were both strangely quiet, facing each other in a fantastic nightmare, while the red sky of dawn was ripped apart with ear-splitting artillery fire. The jungle dust tasted like powder on my lips and the phosphoric odour of the smoke burned my nose and tore at my throat, but I looked straight at the man.

There was a semi-smile on his face. He didn't look as I had expected Nips to look, like the faces of the dead ones I had seen. His face was clean and clear-cut. Sort of simple, and his eyes were wide and brown and somehow honest. Yet there was a hopeless look in them.

I stared at him for a long time. I knew I had to move on.
I knew I couldn't take him prisoner. We didn't have time.
We had to move up and there was no way to let him go.
I raised myself up, inching my head above the edge of the
bomb crater, and looked around. The men were on their
stomachs crawling and behind me more men were coming.
There was nothing I could do. I couldn't let him go back
to his own side and I couldn't take him prisoner. I had to go.

'Hey, Stew!' I heard someone call. 'Stew, you all right?'

I waited a minute without saying anything. Just looking
into the eyes of the man before me. Trying to make myself
hate him. I couldn't answer.

'Hey, Stew!' I heard them call again. 'Are y'all right?'

'Yeh, I'm all right! Be there in a minute,' I yelled back
impatiently. I raised the gun and brought it back to my side
again. I couldn't do it. I thought how much easier it would
be if he would only sneer. But he only looked at me, and
there was a helplessness on his face. He said something in
Japanese.

I couldn't understand, but I knew it was a surrender. He
wanted to surrender. I couldn't take a prisoner. He wasn't
begging me for mercy. His eyes just looked at me. He was
sizing me up as an American, and as a man. He didn't
cringe or sneer, nor did he show any hatred.

'Why, I don't hate this guy,' I thought. 'I can't hate him.'

Another shell went off close and we both ducked. When
we raised up there was a smile on his face. We both laughed.

'God, isn't there some way I can let this guy go,' I thought.
I had shot many a Nip from a distance. That seemed all
right because I had never seen their faces. Only dead ones.

But this man was like a friend. I raised up again and looked out. The men were moving on ahead.

'Hey, Stew!' they called again. 'Come on. We gotta go!'

I knew that I couldn't wait any longer, that I had to go. I raised the gun and I looked at him. He smiled again.

'The guy doesn't even have a fighting chance,' I thought, and wondered wildly about saying, 'All right, get on out.' Let somebody else shoot him. But no, I couldn't do that. He might get behind our lines.

'Hey, Stew!' Rass called. 'Come on, we gotta go!'

The man could see the look I must have had, because he shook his head sadly. He reached for his shirt pocket and pulled out a little board covered with red paper and marked with block Japanese lettering. This, I knew, was the prayer board that all their soldiers carried in battle.

Then I raised the gun, holding it level. His eyes seemed to say, 'So it's true. So it's true what we've been taught about the Americans.' I pulled the trigger.

The shot spat a bright tongue of flame. I crawled up out of the foxhole and started running, moving forward with the men. I didn't want to look back. But I had to. When I did, he was lying there, small and crumpled and still, with that little red-covered piece of wood, that prayer to his gods still in his fingers. He looked peaceful. He looked a lot like the kid Rass had helped die not two hours before.

2

We established the Pilar-Bagac line again and the fighting went on. Sometimes it would be furious for days, and then it would relax and some other portion of the line would

get it. But now most of the desire to fight had been sapped
from me. I could not shake off the murderous feeling of
having killed a helpless man.

During a lull I sat with my friends on the side of a little
hill. All around us other men in the company were either
sleeping or sitting together talking. At the foot of the hill
ran a small stream. It had been a relief to bathe that morning
and wash out socks and shirts. They were dry now, but we
had put them back on wet, for at any moment the shelling
might begin again. Above us towered a huge acacia tree.
Weldon was trying to fix his old World War I Enfield rifle,
which constantly jammed on him.

'I wish I'd brought me a decent gun before I left the
States,' Weldon said, pulling the little piece of oiled gauze
out and laying it on the ground beside him. 'Damn, I was
innocent! I thought the Army was supposed to give a guy
something better than a flintlock to fight with.' I felt he
could have twisted the barrel with his powerful hands in
disgust.

I realized Hughes was looking at me, understanding on
his tired face.

'Sid, you shouldn't let that thing worry you,' he said in
his crisp English accent. 'You shouldn't think about it all
the time.' He was serious and checked his nose-inhaler in
mid-air. 'After all, boy, this is war, and that's just one of
the things of war.'

But I couldn't shake it off. Rass walked over and sat down
next to me.

'Sid wouldn't you like to come here some time when it's
peaceful?' he said. 'Isn't the jungle a pretty thing?'

I looked up. The trees were beautiful and large. The

acacias had roots high as a man's head sticking out like grasshopper legs. It would take eight men with arms outstretched to reach around one of those trees. High up monkeys were chattering noisily, gossiping and pointing down at us. They were funny, and I laughed at them.

'You know, I don't know what makes war,' Rass said solemnly. 'But I'll be hanged if I can see that war's inevitable.'

John interrupted him. 'As long as men are men, and countries are made up of individuals, we'll have wars. Masses of people don't make war. It's individuals that make war.' His voice still had the classroom tone. Since we had had a chance to bathe I knew he was happier. 'It's ambition within every man, an ambition to control other men, that makes it possible to have wars. As long as we're not like a bunch of cows, why, there's always going to be war.'

'When you get it all figured out, you let me know!' one of the boys called over from a little distance. It was Skeeter, a typical hill-billy from the Tennessee mountains. His personality showed through his freckled face, sandy hair and grinning smile. He walked over and sat down with our group.

'The thing worries me mostest is, when do you think they're gonna get us some help? You heard any new rumours lately?'

'Well, the latest I hear is,' Weldon said, 'they say help's only about forty-eight hours away. There's a big convoy just waiting to pull in.'

'Yeh, I know,' Skeeter nodded. 'Anyway that's what Cap'n Jones told me.' He stretched wearily. 'Y'know when they get that help in there, I betcha, I betcha we don't have to fight no more. We been doin' this fer, seems to me, fer a million years,' he said. Then he looked down at a scratch on his leg which was beginning to get infected.

'Funny, I took this little old scratch up there to one of the medics. I guess he was just about all in, 'cause he nearly cried when I showed it to him, and I says, "Y'know, this here damn thing is getting a little infected." And he near cried, cause he says, "Y'know, we haven't got any medicine. We don't even have no quinine any more. And half the guys in this whole outfit are down with malaria."'

'Well, the thing that's worrying me is, what about food?' Hughes put in. 'They didn't give us anything. Yesterday we had four cans of salmon to split between eight men, and that's all we got all day.'

'We haven't had anything today yet,' Rass said.

'Well, it isn't the food I'm thinking about as much as I am about ending up like Gordon did yesterday,' Weldon said.

We were silent for a moment. Gordon, a right guy whose wisecracking had kept us all laughing, had tried to reach a wounded man. He had been killed.

As I thought about him now, I could remember how all of us stood on the bow of the ship as we sailed out from underneath the Golden Gate Bridge. We had all sung as we looked back at the city standing on the hills. We sang at the top of our voices 'Auld Lang Syne.' I thought of his clear Lithuanian voice as he sang. Now he'd rot in the Bataan slime, he'd never go home. I shook off the feeling, for suddenly the Jap trench mortars began opening up.

We crawled back into our foxholes and the attack resumed. I think we held our ground that day. But each day now the attack was more furious, the battle more desperate, and gradually we were forced back.

We dug in again and again, trying to hold, trying vainly to keep from being forced farther down the tiny peninsula of Bataan. There was nothing wrong with our men. I can say that very proudly. But good God, if only we had had anything adequate to fight with. Our stuff, much of it, wasn't even as good as the broomsticks and cornstalks that, I remember somebody saying cynically, Americans have to leap to arms with. My Indian-war sixshooter was one sturdy if not shining exception. We had old, pitted World War I Enfield rifles, trench mortars that were twenty-five years old, and a few antique machine guns that must have belonged first to the Confederates. We were desperately in need of everything. Our hand grenades were old and damp from being buried so many years. You would pull the pin on one and count, and maybe it would never go off. Or maybe it would, too soon, in the vicious way of such things when they get old. We tried to increase our count until many lost an arm from counting too long. There was no way to judge.

We had no planes overhead for protection. Day by day, hours on end, through the night and through the awakening of the day, the Japanese bombed incessantly. They flew with the freedom of no attack, for we had nothing. Our planes had long been destroyed. Our anti-aircraft shells were old and their timers worn out. They would arch into the air and fall back, to explode sometimes just above our heads. They killed far more of us than they did of the Japs.

The native troops that were with us were hungry too and even more poorly equipped than we. Some had no shoes, but they were gallant and brave and hopeful. They were proud of fighting side by side with the Americans. They were sure of the victory that would be theirs. We waited each day and strengthened our hearts for the time when help would come from the States.

Unless a man was terribly wounded, he stayed at his post and fought. There was no more gasoline to haul the wounded back behind the lines. The native troops were our salvation, for they showed us how to eat the roots and berries that grew on the hills.

No man gave up. No man thought of surrendering. We had seen the mutilated bodies of our friends when they fell into Japanese hands. We knew the Japanese were not taking prisoners on the line and we felt sure no prisoners would be taken at all. So we held on for our lives, and prayed and waited for the help that was surely coming from the States.

The day came when our permanent gun emplacements, big one-five-five artillery, stationed high on the mountain tops, were captured by the Japanese. With these in their hands they began to rain down on us a terrific barrage. Our French seventy-fives were inadequate and old, and the ammunition poor and unsure. Our strength was dwindling and our supplies at the vanishing point, but our hopes became stronger. The rumours flew faster and faster.

Every day men made themselves believe the rumours that help was only a few hours away. When those hours passed and help did not come, men again convinced themselves that it was only a matter of a few hours.

There was a perpetual, choking dust, for it was nearly time for the rainy season, and the last bit of moisture was gone. The hard ground was muscle-wracking and the little food that we got sat ill on our stomachs. We suffered heat and flies, dirty feet and the constant roar of the airplane engines. It was a perpetual moving and never settling down, go, go, go, always on the go, night and day and on through the night again and into the day. Today is like tomorrow and tomorrow is like today. They stretch out into one long, dull pattern until you are insensible to feeling, you are one mass of aching flesh, when will it ever stop? 'Oh, God, when will it ever stop, oh, God, I am so tired!'

We think again that help is only a few hours away, even though we fall back, day by day, inching our way back, knowing that if help doesn't come soon we will be pushed into the sea. I'm so tired and hungry, and the food is less than it ever has been. Our chances of getting food every day are now next to impossible, with the planes constantly overhead and the constant barrage of artillery fire bursting about us. The clacking and the tiny buzzing of the machine guns in a constant drum against my brain.

Weary and red-eyed, choking with the constant dust, my friends held together. We received word that Singapore had long since fallen, nearly two months before. We were holding out on Bataan against odds that we all knew. Could we keep on holding out? I began to doubt it, but seeing the determination and hope on the faces of my friends I could not say so. Weldon did not consider for a minute that help would not come. He cursed those who doubted it. Cursing, he would hate himself also for doubting, because doubt made the gnawing fear within himself stronger.

One force about us was stronger than men, the force of nature, the oppressing jungle. To it we didn't matter. We might tear at the trees, destroy some, shell-blast more, leave

gaunt skeletons against the sky, but no matter. Though we
died, though all men died, in a year, possibly two, the scars
would be gone. The jungle would return to itself as though
we had never been there.

But to us it was important to live and fight. The shells
and flares shooting up all around us lit up the night and the
leaves and vines overhead. The monkeys' screaming mingled
with the hoot of the owls. We fell back in the terrific battle
of Abucay, and then Bagak. Soon our entire army was fighting in a little area of about twelve square miles.

We were all front. There was no behind-the-lines now.
There was no place to take the wounded. The Japanese
were trying mercilessly to break our morale. They were
bombing the hospitals. The wounded and the sick were
desperately tired, and had nowhere to turn, nowhere to go.
I remember. . . .

We had lain the whole day in the foxhole, fearing to raise
our heads. The fury of death raged above us and as the
night drew on, we huddled down together. I could hear a
man in one of the foxholes near us praying.

'Oh, God, don't let me die. Take care of me. Don't let
me die, God. Please, God, don't let me die.'

Side by side, Rass and I listened to the man's words. We
were used to our own prayers, seldom audible, but prayers
nevertheless and fervent. Rass spoke up, speculating.

'You know, Sid, I don't believe I've ever heard you come
right out and pray to live. I know that you want to live, but
I have never heard you ask God to let you live.'

'No, Rass, I never have asked God to let me live, and I'll
tell you why.' I looked over at his puzzled face in the faint
light. 'When I was a little boy, at home in Watonga, there

was a hardware store that was giving away a little red car.
You got tickets on this car with every so many purchases at
this store. I have never seen a little car like that since. It
had bicycle tyres and it was big enough for three kids to ride
in it. It had a real gasoline engine, like a washing machine
engine, I guess, because it went "pop, pop, pop."

'Dad and mother saved up the tickets they got. I never
in my life wanted anything like I wanted that little red car.
For a month before the drawing I didn't think a bad thought.
All day long I kept thinking, if I'm real good, God will let
me have that car. I'd pray every night for an hour down on
my knees beside the bed. I'd pray that I'd win that little car.

'Oh, the dreams I had of driving around in that little red
car. It's funny, but mother was running around forcing
tonics down my throat. She was sure I was sick because I
was so darn good. And as the day came closer, I was more
careful for fear I might even think something bad, or do
something bad, and then I wouldn't get that car.

'I'd go down in the afternoons and look at it and run my
hands over it and hear the sound of the motor going "pop,
pop, pop." Then I'd go home and pray for that car.

'Finally the day of the drawing came and I stood with
all the other kids and their folks. My dad had the tickets
all laid out. I waited as a blindfolded little girl ran her hand
down in a cage and drew out a number. When the number
was announced—why dammit, Rass! I didn't get that car.
One of the meanest little kids in town got that car. And he
never did anything good. I felt cheated. I felt that God had
cheated me, Rass, because I didn't win that car.

'As I got older I used to think about it. The worst thing
that could have happened to me was if God had let me win

that car. I learned right then that a man hasn't got a right to ask God for little red cars, because that's not what we're here for. God doesn't go around giving little boys or grown men little red cars just because they ask for them. Men get little red cars because they work.

'Since then I've seen so many die. Good guys too, Rass, guys that believed in God stronger than I do. When I see those guys die, I think, well, life's a luxury. Even if it isn't a luxury I haven't got any right to ask God to live. I'm not going to ask him for a little red car. With all these shells bursting around me I've got the feeling that my life is just like that little red car.'

My mind flew back to the day the war started and the prayer I had made after seeing the wounded lying in the hospital yard. God had given me what I asked for and Rass knew about that prayer. Things in my personality too weak for my control I had begged God to help me with. But life, no. It was a tangible, precious thing that I wanted with every breath. But hadn't better men than I died praying to live? And God is great and I knew He wept for them and suffered with their pain.

'I do ask God to give me strength to take all this, to be a better man and to help me make myself a better man. If God wants me to live, if He's got anything He wants me to do with my life, He'll help me do it. If He wants me to live, He'll let me. But I'm not going to ask for any little red cars.'

Darkness had already covered the skies and they were lit now with man-made stars that burst and sent their deadly sparks hurtling toward the earth. There was a pungent burning smell, and the cries of wounded men. Rass turned over on his side.

'I have faith in God to give me anything I ask for,' he said firmly. 'I don't look on life like that. I'm going to go on and ask God to let me live.' Then he gripped me by the arm. 'Sid, we'll make it all right together.'

Soon he was asleep. I lay there awhile listening to the sounds of the war and the cries of the birds, long kept awake. And beyond in the distance, the frightened chattering of the monkeys. I waited for the morning.

3 Fall of Bataan: April 1942

AT LAST we received no more food at all. The fury of the fighting made it impossible to deliver what rations we might have had. Our front line was pushed back and back by the Japanese onslaught, gradually crowding us toward the sea. Malaria and dengue fever, diarrhoea, hunger and weariness tore at our ranks. The unrelenting sun was like an open furnace glaring in the sky, and the unburied dead lay bloating and yellow over the battle ground.

Communications were gone. Our artillery was almost on the infantry line. We began to admit openly that help from the States might not reach us in time. Ammunition was running short. We had plenty of big ammunition, but we had lost all of our larger artillery to the Japanese. Every ounce of the smaller stuff was precious now. Each shot had to count.

At night the jungle became a horrible thing. The huge artillery shells guttered their way through the sky and then burst into man-made daylight. Also, we were frightened by smaller things. The Jap planes dropped packages of firecrackers behind our lines. They exploded like ripping machine-gun fire. They made us feel we were surrounded. We were tired, exhausted, and the days were long. Could we hold out?

The end came on April 8th, 1942. One of the men from a nearby Company rushed to us.

'It's happened!' he yelled hysterically. 'The Fifty-First has given way. Their lines are broken. They're running for their lives, and the Twenty-Sixth has given way on the other side. What'll we do? Where'll we go?'

We sat stunned. The worst is never truly expected, regardless of how long the mind is gauged for it. Hope throws up a blind wall that cuts off the most skilled imagination. Hughes sat with his mouth open, staring at Weldon as though begging him to deny this thing. But the powerful miner was drained of speech. He kept glaring at the sky and spitting at the ground as though he had tasted a bitter acid. Only John was outwardly unmoved by the terrible news. An hour before he had been quoting poetry to us with more feeling than he showed now. I wondered if long ago he had given up all hope of returning to his classrooms at the University of Wisconsin.

Rass' face was deadly white in the exploding light, but his dark eyes seemed to be searching for a way out. Our last officer had been killed that morning and we had nowhere to turn for authority or direction. Every sergeant held his men together through each man's frightened desire to be told what to do. Men hoped to keep their minds a blank against terrifying reality. The indecision broke like a river dam, and everyone began talking and yelling at once.

'Maybe,' Weldon said, his voice gathering hope, 'we'd better try to get all of us together and cut through the jungle side of the mountain and make it to Marivales.'

'Maybe we could get to Corregidor,' Rass said quickly, pushing back his unruly hair.

Somehow I knew Corregidor could not take us all. There were too many on Bataan. It would be like a lifeboat whose occupants had to fight to keep too many men from getting into it when it was full. I started to tell them. Then I bit my tongue. It wasn't a time to talk. We had to get out. We had to do something.

'My God, I wonder what'll happen to us if we don't make it though.' There was horror on Hughes' face. His English accent added to the unreality.

I knew what he was thinking of. Yesterday we had found the body of one of our men. His hands and feet were cut off, and bayonets were driven into his stomach. We found the body lying there in the sun as the Nips had left it. We knew they weren't taking any prisoners.

I sat there paralysed. Weldon jumped up and yelled to the other men. Then he worked his way to each one of the foxholes telling them the news. We waited, speechless and stunned, until he crawled back into the foxhole with us.

'They're all game to try to make it to Corregidor,' he said grimly. 'So we'd better start.'

Somehow, like sleepless zombies, we started making our way back through the jungle. No man spoke of the thoughts that were in his mind. We moved slowly, certain that movement, any movement, was better than sitting still waiting for it to come. So we moved back, making our way through the jungle.

Darkness fell quickly in the jungle. The night was lit with a million flares that burst in the sky above us. The earth began to shake and reverberate as the ammunition dumps exploded. It was a nightmare in hell. The end of the world had come. I reached forward and gripped Rass' arm, wanting to feel the reality of someone near me. As the ammunition dumps went, the stark trees shook and danced to the roaring blasts. You could read a book by the lurid glare of the constant explosions. The artillery pounded away and shell fragments screamed through the air. The demolition of unused aeroplane bombs vomited diabolic destruction, shaking the ground like an earthquake.

We went on through the jungle and down the mountain-side like frightened lost children. I felt as if I were hiding beneath an iron tub and giants were beating the sides with huge stone mallets. With each blow the sparks cast themselves down upon me, searing into my brain.

We came to a little clearing on the hillside. The men threw themselves down and rested without speaking. No one dared to speak for fear of letting loose a chain of emotions within himself. Each man sensed the fear within his companions. We had a horrible feeling of loss and loneliness. Loneliness, for death we knew was coming. And death strikes each man as an individual. You are alone, no matter how many are there.

We lay still, watching the flares and feeling the trembling of the ground beneath us.

'All right, you guys.' I heard Weldon's gruff voice. 'We're not going to lie here all night. We gotta get going.'

'Going where?' someone said. 'We might as well stay here and face it.'

'Aw, shut up!' someone else snarled. 'You don't know what's going to happen.'

I understood for a moment that strong rationalization in every man's mind. With the inevitable right upon us, some were refusing to accept it.

We crawled slowly to our feet. Staggering, we started back through the jungle and down the mountainside until we reached a road. In the flares the white coral road was like a white ribbon that stretched down to the beach.

Ahead of us we could see the city of Marivales and the native grass shacks, aburst with flame like giant torches. Their flames danced like mad sprites against the darkness of the sea behind. By now we were surrounded by thousands of other men. Their faces showed wide eyes and mouths tight with fear. None of them knew where he was going, but cattle-like followed the man ahead.

We wandered down to the beach. Waiting, hoping against hope, waiting. Still the planes crashed their bombs from overhead and the artillery gutted among us. The men no longer sought protection. As the pieces of shrapnel screamed by our ears there was something almost comforting about the sound. Wouldn't it be better to die now than to face what we were sure awaited us?

'Tell everyone to get rid of their souvenirs!' someone passed the word. 'Get rid of everything you have that the Japanese might suspect belonged to their troops.'

Stupidly, I wondered why. We gathered what was left of our Company and built a little fire on the beach and the Company records were burned. Then each man came forward and emptied his papers upon it.

It was a small fire, an insignificant speck against the giant flares and the burning city below us. How small, but how important it was. As its flames danced, it reduced to ashes all records of what we were and who we were. Then the Company flag was brought forward and laid on the

fire and I turned my face and looked back toward the jungle.
I could not stand to see those colours burning. Suddenly I
heard Weldon crying beside me, and the sobs shook his body.

'The Americans didn't even try to send us help,' he choked.
'They deserted us.'

I turned to comfort him but he didn't need me. Hughes,
always the weakest of our party, the most easily frightened,
stood there holding his arm, patting his back, encouraging
him. Then I saw two men carry forward the American flag.
They opened it and shook it out in the wind.

In the flares, the bright red-and-white stripes and the
little stars in the blue background danced for a moment.
Soon it would be a memory of what we stood for. They let
one corner of the flag touch the little fire. The flames licked
up through the red and white stripes toward the blue. I
noticed that all the men were crying, and I could feel the
tears as they fell on my cheeks. I gritted my teeth, almost
hating America. Hating America who had left us here.

'We fought all this time, thinking that America would send
us help,' John said.

It was hard for me to watch him cry. He complained so
seldom. I knew what the burning of that flag meant to him
and to the men standing around me.

When the last sparkle of it had been reduced to white
ashes, we lay down exhausted on the sand of the beach and
waited for the morning light, but we did not sleep. Each
man stared silently at the sky, clutching his own thoughts,
examining his own soul, waiting for what the sun and the
day and the Japanese Army would bring.

'I'll bet if my mother knew about this, she'd sure raise

hell!' one man spoke up. Everyone roared with laughter. It felt good, that laughter. It released the tension within us and every man felt better.

As the morning light glistened its way across the water below me I heard one man talking to another.

'General King has gone forward on the road carrying a white flag,' he said flatly. 'But don't nobody reckon they'll let us surrender.'

The order to destroy our guns was passed among us, no man knowing whence it came. We set about the procedure as we had been taught.

'This old thing ain't never been any good,' Weldon said slowly, running his fingers over the stock of the old Enfield rifle like a mother caressing a child. 'Be plain sabotage to let some Nip have an ornery gun like you.'

John kept staring at the smoke rising from the ruins of Marivales, only his eyes alive in the white delicate face. 'Even now the devastation has begun, and half the business of destruction done,' he quoted from Goldsmith's *Deserted Village*, as though he stood all alone searching for beauty in a world falling apart before his eyes, a world that bewildered him. Tears came into my eyes and I wiped them on my dirty sleeve.

Rass laid his hand on my arm. I hadn't realized till then how I was trembling. His face was drawn and tired, but his eyes were dry and he tried desperately to smile.

'Don't think they'll let us surrender.' His lips trembled and he looked away, then back. 'Never did get to tell you about a horse I had once.'

I didn't listen. The flares no longer brightened in the morning light, but their smoke snaked through the sky. The dust from the road just above me was thick, and mingled with the fumes like white powder. As I looked at the faces of the men I felt a tight binding within me. I jerked my eyes away and looked back to the mountains. Mount Bataan with its cool crater, stretched away into the high blue sky. It was unperturbed, untouched by the tiny men who crawled like ants over its sides. Soon I saw strange tanks rumbling down the road, the dust rising beside them like smoke.

Japanese soldiers were coming out of the brush. They walked to the edge of the road and stood looking down at us. I expected at any moment to feel machine-gun bullets ripping through my flesh. The tanks stopped and the turrets were opened. I saw one Japanese officer raise himself up. He stood on the inside of the tank, looking over the turret at the bedraggled, heartbroken army. A smile lit his lips, a smile of triumph. Then he screamed orders to the Japanese soldiers.

'They want us to move up on to the road,' said a voice. 'They want us all to come up and bring all of our stuff.'

We struggled to our feet.

'Let's all stick together,' Rass suggested. 'Whatever happens, it'll be easier to take it that way.'

We started walking toward the road, not knowing what was to happen.

2

We reached the road and the Japanese motioned haughtily for us to stand in the depressions along the sides of the old coral highway. Holding their rifles flat and ready, they moved among us slowly, coolly suspicious, their eyes glaring.

With the gasping breath of relief the word was passed

along, 'They're going to make us prisoners.' Suddenly the deafening roar of the explosions stopped. All firing ceased.

The quick silence was an odd sound to our ears, so used to the war. An occasional rifle shot cracked in the distance, ringing with a hollow echo over the jungle. When I looked at the dust-covered faces of our captors, I felt the cold hatred in their eyes, and wondered how we would be treated. We laid our stuff out on the ground in front of us and unrolled our packs. Most of us had very little, as a soldier throws everything away but the very essential.

The Japanese officers walked back and forth in the road, their samurai swords clacking against their black boots. By contrast the Jap enlisted men were dressed in patched and ragged uniforms and wrapped to the knees in puttees like those the American soldiers had worn in the First World War. An order was screamed in Japanese. I don't know why we all looked at John, expecting him to translate for us. But of course he couldn't. The Japs began knocking our helmets off with the tips of their bayonets. They fell to the ground with the clamour of tin wash pans.

'You don't have any Japanese souvenirs, do you?' John asked me out of the corner of his mouth.

'No, I got rid of everything,' I whispered.

The Jap guards began to feel us over, searching us. I had a little medical kit strapped to my belt. A Japanese soldier, half grinning, ripped it from my belt and emptied it upon the ground. Grunting, he stooped forward and picked up a bottle of Sodium Amytal, a potent sleeping medicine. Each green tablet contained three grains. He looked into my face with contempt and hatred in his eyes, questioning me. Then he uncorked the bottle and poured the tablets out into his hand.

'*Yoroshi?* Are they good?' He asked in Japanese. I looked at him, sensing his feeling of superiority and hating him for it.

'*Tien yoroshi,*' I said, remembering the words I had learned from a prisoner we had taken. He poured a few more into his hand. 'Yes,' I repeated. 'They are very good.'

Lifting his hand to his mouth, he gulped them down and walked to the next man and began searching him. I felt a small triumph. I knew he would live only a few minutes. He would not vomit because they would act as a sedative. Slowly he would fall asleep and die. I felt glad of it as I looked at the glaring mahogany faces of our captors. They didn't know it yet, but I had notched one more to our score, right under their noses.

'Just look at these poor guys,' Rass whispered. I looked around at the Filipinos and the Americans lined up in the road. Their faces were half-starved and dirty from the swirling chalky dust of the coral road glaring in the sun. Their clothes were in rags and there was fear and hatred in their tired red eyes. They were expecting something very bad and now it was coming.

Suddenly the Japanese soldiers began to lose restraint. They jerked off watches and fountain pens. Then they lost their tempers, slugging and beating the men up and down the line. A boy who stood near me cried out with pain as one of the Jap guards smashed a fist into his face. The guard laughed, then raised the butt of his rifle, crashing it down over the boy's head. Groaning, the kid sagged to his knees. With all his strength the guard swung the butt again and the boy's head made a dull, splattering sound as it split open before our eyes.

The body convulsed, shuddering, and the fingers grabbed

the ground. Then it lay still. One of the Jap soldiers laughed and kicked the dead American with the toe of his shoe. Suddenly I hated them with a violent hatred.

Never had I wanted to kill for the sheer pleasure of killing before. But now, good God, how I wanted to tear them limb from limb. I despised myself for the times when I had felt sorry for them.

'The dirty bastards!' Weldon was rasping through set teeth.

'Shut up!' John's whisper was firm. 'This is no time to lose your head. Hold your temper and take it easy. You don't want to end up like that guy!' The black hatred still boiled in my brain, but gradually I got control of myself.

'Yahura!' the guards began to yell. 'Start moving!'

We started out on the road, leaving our little handful of possessions behind us. Every few yards more Japanese materialized from the bushes around us. We were covered by the white dust stirred up by the horse-drawn artillery and the trucks. Jap soldiers, as they filed along, would jerk an American out of line and beat him, then shove him back into the line. There was no reason in the performance. They did it purely for entertainment.

Before we had gone two miles our shirts were stripped from our bodies. The sun reached straight above us, beating down on our bare heads. My head began to ache in the blistering heat. My eyes seemed to bulge from my head. I wanted water more than anything. We kept walking and the heat seemed to search out all the strength in me.

'Oh, God, where are we going? Where are we going?' Hughes whimpered. John gave him a savage 'Sshh!'

The afternoon wore on and the Japanese soldiers lining

the road became more ferocious. The sun beat on my head
and it ached almost to splitting with the heat of it. My skin
felt pierced by a million needles of fire. I passed a man lying
in the road with his head smashed in, and then another,
writhing in misery, clutching his belly in bloody hands. A
bayonet had been driven through his intestines. Soon it
became commonplace and I saw scores and finally hundreds
like them. I began to think only of lifting my feet one at a
time and putting them down.

'Keep up, Sid,' Weldon said grimly. 'Keep up, don't be
falling back. I hear they're going to let us rest up ahead.'

'They'll have trucks up there to move us out,' someone
passed the word. Just the thought refreshed me. They were
going to put us on trucks, surely, and we would have
water.

Slowly the darkness fell. The coolness of night descended.
I watched men fall to the ground. The Japanese rushed in
among us, kicking them with their heavy boots and jabbing
them with their bayonets. If the men could not rise they
were beaten to death. My hatred gave me strength. Then I
remembered the Jap who had taken the Sodium Amytal
from my medical kit. I began to laugh hysterically.

Rass reached over and shook me. 'What's wrong, fella?
Hold on. What's wrong?'

'I got one of the bastards, Rass. I got one of the bastards.'

'Get hold of yourself, Sid.' John gripped my shoulder.

'I got one of the bastards, the dirty bastards.' I laughed
hysterically. In a whisper I told them how the Jap had swallowed twenty of the Sodium Amytal tablets.

'Won't he vomit them up?' Hughes asked.

'No, he won't.' Rass shook his head. 'He'd just fall over

and sleep and pretty soon he'd be dead. Oh, God, if we only could give it to them alll'

We laughed at that and it helped.

We walked all night and when the dawn came it brought the sun again. The temperature rose slowly as the sun climbed in the sky. The noon hour came and the midday heat was blistering, searing our skins. But we straggled on, afraid to fall by the side. The heat and the choking dust filled our noses, tearing at our raw throats.

Hughes kept stumbling and whimpering. He walked bent almost in half and the white coral dust covering his hair gave him the appearance of a very old man. John, who never complained, began a rasping cough and his dirt mask was criss-crossed with lines of running sweat.

During the afternoon we came to a cool mountain stream and the Japanese yelled for us to stop. We stood there, knowing we were to get water. The dampness of the ground smelled mossy and wonderful. Looking down at the cool stream bubbling and gurgling over the rocks, I licked my cracked and gritty lips. It looked so clear, so cool, so delicious. If only I could throw myself down into the water and lie there feeling it rush over my body.

We waited and waited, but still they did not allow us to drink. Suddenly one of the men could bear it no longer. He rushed forward, fell on his hands and knees, threw his face into the water. A Japanese non-com ran up, unsheathing his sword and swinging it high.

I heard a quick, ugly swish. Before I could realize what had happened, I saw the head roll away in the stream. The blood and water mingled together, a violent red. The body was stationary for a moment and suddenly the blood gushed

out of the gaping hole at the neck like a waterfall. The body
lunged forward in the stream bed, the hands opening and
closing. Feeling sick, I thought, 'It is like a chicken with its
neck wrung.' I hated myself for the thought. I closed my
eyes and gritted my teeth.

The guards yelled for us to go on. They were not going
to let us have water. Without stopping or turning we headed
up the dusty road glaring in the tropical sun.

'I don't think I can make it much farther,' I heard Hughes
whisper. 'I don't feel like I can make it another block.'

'I don't think I can either,' Rass gasped. But then a mile
passed.

'Just keep thinking that you're gonna get water up ahead,'
Weldon begged, the strength almost gone from his deep
voice.

I began to fasten my mind on the thought of water, how
good it would taste. My mouth was terribly dry and my
tongue felt rough and swollen in my mouth. The dust tasted
gritty on my cracked lips. I licked my tongue across them,
thinking of water and its taste. Somehow the night passed
and the morning sun came again. I remembered passing
through Orion and then Pilar.

The sun beat down on my throbbing head. I thought only
of bringing my feet up, putting them down, bringing them
up. Along the road the jungle was a misty green haze, swimming before my sweat-filled eyes.

The hours dragged by, and a great many of the prisoners
reached the end of their endurance. The drop-outs became
more numerous. They fell by the hundreds in the road.
Some made an effort to rise. Groaning and weeping, they
tried to get to their feet. Some succeeded, others fell back

helplessly. I wondered that the Jap guards paid no attention. Why? Why did they leave them, when they had killed them before?

Suddenly I knew. There was the crack of a pistol and the shot rang out across the jungle. There was another shot, and more shots, and I knew that, straggling along behind us, was a clean-up squad of Japanese, killing their helpless victims on the white dusty road. The shots rang out through the night, making orange flashes in the darkness. I wondered how soon our bodies would be with the rest. The shots continued, goading us on. I gritted my teeth. 'Oh, God, I've got to keep going. I can't stop. I can't die like that.'

When morning came, John said, 'I can't make it this day. I cannot make it.'

'I can't either, John.'

But we kept on and the sun climbed slowly higher and higher. We passed thousands of American and Filipino bodies bloating and rotting in the sun.

At noon they stopped us. There was a flurry of activity up ahead. There were carabao holes beside the road, like pig wallows, with greenish water and slimy scum covering the top. Small gnats and flies buzzed around them. Even so, it was water.

We looked, asking the question with our eyes of our Jap guards. Surprisingly, they nodded, and we ran for it. Falling on our knees, we pushed the scum back from the top of the water with our hands. The stenching liquid was water. When we started down the road again, somehow I felt better.

The murders went on. Death was always at our heels. We struggled to keep going. Weldon pushed Hughes with his shoulder, trying to keep him from falling. Rass half-carried John at times. Then he would shift him to me. We would change positions and I would walk in front with John's hands on my shoulders, holding him up.

On the fifth day we arrived at Orani. They herded us on to the cement patio of an old Spanish church. They motioned for us to sit down, but we were so crowded that we had to sit with our knees hunched up in front of us. After a little while huge caldrons of steaming rice were brought forward and a small handful was ladled out to each one of us. We ate ravenously. But no sooner had we finished eating than the guards ran in among us, screaming, kicking us with their boots, making us get to our feet.

The rest had cramped my muscles and my legs jerked with the effort as we started up the road. Gradually I began to lose consciousness. I was surrounded by a scorching, thirsty haze. My eyes grew dim and I thought only of keeping my feet moving. I had to keep going. Walking, Walking. I no longer noticed when the men in my Company fell out. No longer counted the bodies in the road.

Sometime late in the night we started through the outskirts of the Filipino city of Lubao. It may have been a day later, for Weldon told me we had been walking for eight days. In Lubao the Filipinos stood at the open windows of their homes and threw food to us. A scramble started among the prisoners. I watched them through a haze, wondering how they had the strength to fight. The guards screamed in frenzy, stamping and grinding the food under their feet, and beating a man if he picked up a piece of it.

We were herded on through the streets of the city, much like the other cities, with bamboo homes set on stilts. At the end of one street there was an ancient Alamo-style church.

My eyes burned with the sun and sweat and dust, but when
I looked at the compassion and pity on the faces of the
Filipinos I became more determined. I will go on, I thought.
I'll live to see these bastards die.

Somehow we reached the other side of the city. They
marched us into an open field. An interpreter screamed
that we were not to sit down. The nerves in my legs began
an uncontrollable jerking and I wondered what we were
waiting for. Weldon stood as though propped up by some
unseen force, his eyes staring without focus. Hughes leaned
against him with his knees sagging. His once-blond hair was
muddy with sweat and dust, and his face was drawn and
cadaverous. John swayed drunkenly, his hand gripping Rass'
shoulder. Rass' bloodshot eyes grew suddenly alive. I followed the look in them.

A guard walked by with an American head stuck on the
end of his bayonet. My stomach turned over at the sight.
Blood was running from the neck and from the open lips.
The teeth were clenched in a ghastly smile and the eyes
protruded. I turned my eyes away, but I saw three other
Japs, each of them with an American head on a bayonet.
They walked in among us and we fell silent, watching them
with black, deadly hatred.

Night came at last, yet we continued to stand there. If a
man slumped to his knees the guards rushed in, jabbing him
with their bayonets or kicking him until he either stood or
fell groaning to the ground.

When morning came we started again. The day was like
the rest, horribly hot and thirsty. But we walked and the
day passed and the night passed.

'We're on the outskirts of San Fernando,' Rass said. His

voice sounded like an echo in a cave. 'They'll give us food
here. They're going to put us on a train.'

I shook my head. I could not trust myself to speak. I did
not believe it. The only thing that gave me hope was the
fact that they didn't kill us. They must have some reason
for marching us, goading us, beating us on like this. Surely
somewhere was the end of this trail of blood and death.

'We've been walking nine days now,' John said. The words
rasped from his parched throat.

We went on through the streets of San Fernando. My
head was bursting under the constant glare of the sun, and
I lost consciousness. When my head cleared again I was on
a boxcar.

'I don't know what happened to you. I dragged you that
last two miles,' Rass said quietly. 'You kept falling. You
were kicked and beaten but you always managed to get back
on your feet.'

I looked around. John and Weldon and Hughes were
still there. They sat holding their heads in their hands. The
jolting and jarring of the boxcar wracked every muscle in
my body. I looked down. My feet were wet with blood.

On April 21st, twelve days after our surrender, we reached
Camp O'Donnell. It was said that more than fourteen thousand men died on the march. The living also were dying
men at the end, haunted by fear, eaten by pain and fever.

Sometimes I think we all died on the march. Sometimes
I feel sure that all the things that came later were just a
fevered dream, and that somewhere back on those blood-
soaked miles there is another body. . . .

4 Camp O'Donnell, Luzon: May 1942

WE HAD been at Camp O'Donnell five days and more men had died there through the exhaustion and beatings of the long Death March. But the bodies were not buried.

The horrible smell of rotting flesh hung in the air around the camp. It clogged our nostrils and made our eyes water. It clung to the ground like a thick, pungent gas. Through the almost liquid odour came the crying and groans of dying men, the howling of wild dogs in the distance, and the eternal humming buzz of millions of black and blue blowflies. They danced and hung suspended in the haze and humid heat.

We had no way to bury the dead. There were no tools even to dig latrines. Most of the men had dysentery and in their weakened condition they were seldom able to make it outside the shacks.

Hughes lay on the dirt floor of the shack beside us. His hair was matted and flat from the sweat of his fever. His face was pinched and flushed, and his eyes glazed with pain. Weldon sat beside him, holding his hand, mute, helpless, wanting to make his suffering easier.

I reached for our water container and walked out of the hut for water. The camp was large, dotted by hundreds of grass and bamboo shacks, which were merely poles of bamboo with a grass roof. The ground flowed and undulated through the camp in tiny hills. Beside each of the shacks were stacks of bodies pulled there by the living, for they had nowhere else to put them. In the hot tropical sun the bodies swelled and bloated until they were no longer recognizable as the bodies of men. They were just yellow balloon-like forms. Over them swarmed hundreds of black flies and maggots.

I headed on up the hill toward the water faucet that served our section of the camp. There were only three water faucets inside the camp area to serve thousands of men. Water was rationed to one container per man.

Other men walked up the hill toward the water faucet. They looked at the ground, shuffling their feet. None of them talked. There were no smiles, no happiness, just the beaten looks of dying men. Out of their blank eyes came a stare of detachment, of receding within themselves, trying desperately not to be a part of all that was around them. Each of us felt that if he faced the reality of his surroundings, he would die. Over us hung the sky, as brilliantly blue as only a tropical sky can be. The tireless sun glared at the earth.

A Jap guard stood at the end of the line near the water faucet. My eyes fell on his crooked, hunched back. His black, beady eyes looked out of a sunburned face. After the years of the war in China the Japanese were hard put to it for men. For the war with America and Britain they had called every available man to the colours. This one certainly was the bottom of the barrel.

In Japanese psychology it was not very honourable to

guard prisoners. All our guards were misfits, deformed, alcoholic, insane. Depravities of all types stood guard around us, hating us and hating the world because of themselves. I thought of the day we entered the camp. The Japanese officer in charge had made us stand for an hour in the sun while he ranted like a maniac.

'You are the enemies of Nippon,' he screamed in broken English. 'We fight a righteous war, and though we fight a hundred years until our grandsons and our great-grandsons have fought you, we will win. You are not honourable prisoners of war. You are captives and you shall be treated as captives.'

While he spoke, John muttered the old nursery rhyme, 'Oh, sticks and stones may break my bones, but words shall never hurt me'.

'The dirty bastard,' Weldon grunted. 'The stupid fool.'

As I looked at the blank masks of the American prisoners around me I wanted to scream, 'Can't you see what these men are, these guards? How can you let them do this to you? Look at them and feel superior'.

But the sun was hot and I was silent like the rest. Shuffling along with them in the line I felt that I was the only man alive in the group. These were the mythical zombies. They cared not for themselves, nor for the death that was coming.

A hand was laid on my shoulder, and it felt cool against my burning flesh.

'I've been watching you, son,' a remembered voice said. I swung about, incredulous. Then I recognized him.

My heart jumped with delight. Father Cummings after so many months! I couldn't believe it. He had suffered, I could see, but his face still radiated an unalterable goodness and gentleness. His sandy hair was nearly white and he had grown unbelievably thin. The deeply-tanned skin was pulled tight over his skull, and his peaceful, kindly eyes were set in cavernous sockets. His clothes were in rags. The old khaki shirt had no sleeves and revealed his brown, bony arms. It was a sharp contrast to the flowing white tropical habit he had worn the night we had left the old castle.

'I haven't seen you since we left Manila that night together,' I said, gripping his hand hard. 'How have you been?'

'I've worked very hard, Sid, but I have loved my work.' His voice still held a quiet intimacy and understanding. He looked around at the men and I followed his eyes, knowing how his heart went out to them. I remembered something from before the surrender, and I tried to change the subject.

'Father, they say you've become famous all over the world for your statement that there are no atheists in foxholes. They quote it now, they say, in the newspapers all over America.'

He didn't answer me. I don't think he even heard. He kept staring at the silent, hopeless faces of the prisoners around him.

'I must work harder,' he said with a sigh. 'These men need me.'

Taking my eyes from his face I looked back toward the camp behind me, and then again to the men around us. The words slipped out without thinking.

'Look at us today, and everything that's going on all around,' I said bitterly. 'I can't understand that this exists and that there can be a God.'

Father Cummings shut his eyes for a minute. His features were tired, as though he carried a terrible torment and the burden of many men's souls.

'It's only with God that everything becomes comprehensible,' he said simply.

His eyes were not on me. I felt that he would do anything to bring rest to the dying faces around us.

'I want to believe in God,' I said. Then I saw the red mahogany face of the Jap guard just ahead, and I gritted my teeth. 'But it's too damned convenient for these sons-of-bitches to pay up in the next world. I want to see justice on earth. I want—'

A firm grip on my arm checked my outburst. 'I'll come down to you this evening,' he said, 'when it's cooler and the sun is going down. I'll come and we'll talk. I think you need to talk.'

Slowly the sun released its scorching grasp upon the earth. Already the spotlights sprayed across the barbed wire fences. Jap guards slouched in the shadows, and from the silhouetted jungle came the cries of wild dogs begging for our unburied dead. Father Cummings' face glowed in the last rays of the setting sun while he talked.

He spoke of God simply, directly. He became a real presence beside us. We felt Him there.

Father Cummings used no dramatic oratory.

'It is a simple thing of faith,' he said tenderly. 'A thing to believe in, to hold to.'

My friends listened quietly. Their eyes showed the longing each had for the tangible human things that only faith could bring again. For John, the lakes of Wisconsin and his classroom. For Hughes, his desperate longing to see an English springtime. Though I could not see Weldon's face, I knew that that powerful, restrained man dreamed of freedom. Only Rass, brushing his hair back off his forehead, seemed to follow the priest's words. I wondered what it was in Father Cummings' voice that reminded me of the brisk wind caressing the red Oklahoma hills of my childhood.

'And though we should soon die, and be stacked with that pile of bodies ourselves,' he said, holding his hand over his mouth to keep out the black flies, 'is it not best to have God at our side? It is a lonely thing,' he went on, 'to die all alone, feeling no presence beside you, feeling that no one cares. I work with the men to let them know that I care, that God cares that they are in pain and dying. If you have faith and you believe, you are never alone. You cannot be lonely, even if you die.' He looked up at the sky and was silent for a moment. In his eyes there was a terrible sadness.

'There are so many men here. I cannot help them all, but if I can help a few, then maybe God will feel my life is justified. When I worry about their suffering, I don't have time to think of myself.' He laid his hand on my arm and looked deep into my eyes. 'The weak will become weaker and the strong will become stronger.' He looked at each of my friends, impressing them with the same thought. Suddenly I felt my life depended on helping the others.

When Father Cummings left us for the night Hughes looked better, and his fever was nearly gone. We sat for an hour without talking, and then we dozed off.

Morning came, with the sickly-sweet odour of rotting human flesh stronger than it had ever been before. Flies seemed to come from everywhere, millions of them swarming in the air. I walked out of the building and stood in the

morning sun. Men were carrying the dead out of the shacks.
The stack of bodies grew. Each day more died, until the
thousands of bodies formed a wall within the camp. The
stench—I do not like to remember it.

The men grew mean as they weakened. The stronger
became sullen and selfish. When the weak cried for water,
the strong brought them none. When the handfuls of worm-
eaten rice we were given each day were passed around, men
stole it from those too weak to fight for their rights.

The days passed. The five of us stuck together, Rass and
Weldon, John and Hughes and myself. When one of us
sank down in illness, eaten with malaria or dysentery, the
rest of us helped him. We tried to help the others around us.
Trying to forget ourselves, we talked to them, carried them
water, brought them food. We continually dreamt of food
ourselves. We lay down at night and thought of food, and
it kept us from sleeping. When we slept we dreamt of
delicious platters of eggs, or of huge steaks, or of exotic
delicacies.

My mouth watered when I woke up, more miserable than
ever. Then I would try to sleep again.

Within twenty days, twenty-three thousand Filipinos and
Americans died. Their bodies were stacked inside the compound. Vultures hovered in the sky, dropping straight down
to the stacks, tearing at the flesh and at the eyes of the
bodies. They watched the yellowed and shrunken skeletons
of the living with greedy eyes.

Soon diet-deficiency diseases ran riot among us. Men had
scurvy. Their teeth fell out and their lips swelled and their
gums bled painfully. Many men could no longer walk because of beri-beri. Thousands had dysentery and passed
blood, screaming with cramps, begging for mercy, praying

to die, and as they died, cursing the things they had believed in.

One evening as I was lying on the floor resting, I heard a familiar voice, low in prayer. I sat up and saw Father Cummings at the end of the building, kneeling beside a boy. He laid his hands on the boy's head.

'In the name of the Father, and of the Son, and of the Holy Ghost.' He baptized the boy with a little of his own ration of water.

I walked over and stood for a moment beside him. The boy's eyes followed the priest in almost worshipful silence. There was a flush in his cheeks as though he had received a transfusion of blood and strength. Father Cummings patted him on the arm.

'You'll be all right, son,' he said. 'I'll come to you again later this evening.' He started to walk out of the building, smiling.

'Father, may I walk with you on your rounds?'

His face lit up. 'Certainly,' he said.

We walked along between the buildings, stopping every so often. Father Cummings would stand at the end of a building and pray for the men. Then he would go in and ask if there was anyone who would like to talk to him.

The men were not all Catholics. There were men of every faith, and men who had no faith at all before he came. Yet he had time for them all. When he bent and touched their foreheads, or gripped their hands, they no longer cried or raved. They grew quiet and their eyes held a new hope.

I wanted to tell Father Cummings how much he was doing for the men, but he stopped me with a gesture.

'As I stand close to these men, so near to dying, I feel

sometimes,' he said, 'that in reality they are closer to God than I am. I feel humble in their presence, for soon they will be with Him. The little I do for them is not as much as I feel it should be.'

How much more could he give? I thought. He wasn't a big man. He wasn't strong. He received no more water than we did, and no more food, and even these he gave away. Yet he censured himself for not giving more. How could he give more and live?

'You remember the story of the Good Samaritan,' he said, and I nodded my head. 'Well, in the story of the Good Samaritan, who do you think took away the greatest gift —the Good Samaritan or the poor man who received his help?'

He knew without my answering that I understood. But he must also have seen something else in my eyes, for he smiled and laid his thin hand on my arm. In the orange brightness of the fence spotlights his eyes became dreamy.

'Stew,' he said seriously, 'I can't sleep some nights for dreaming about plates of fried chicken livers and cold sliced tomatoes.' He turned then and left me, walking slowly towards his own quarters.

I felt a little surprised at his last remark, but as I walked toward our shack I stopped suddenly, smiling to myself. He had wanted me to know that he was only human, too.

2

At last the rains came, toward the end of May. The season I looked forward to with eagerness arrived with a tropical difference. The first black cloud moved down out of the jungle mountains like a gigantic hawk. The rain drummed with ever-increasing momentum against the waxy leaves. The rain's roar could be heard for minutes before the shadow of the cloud reached us, with the crescendo of a waterfall. Just as suddenly, it was gone. But more rain came, until the sky pressed down upon us and we thought it would rain for ever. The ground, which had been dry and powdery, turned to a sloshy, oozing tropical mud.

By now 50 per cent of the men in the camp were dead.

The rain, though it brought relief from the torrid heat, only added to our misery, for the grass shacks were too poorly constructed to hold out water. We shivered in the cold at night, huddling against one another to keep warm. Through the day we trudged up the hill for water, or tried to catch the rain as it fell. Each day, knee-deep in the mud, we dragged the bodies outside. But at last the Japanese themselves tired of the stench and allowed us to have tools to dig graves. There were few strong enough to carry the dead. The rotted bodies were taken to the edge of the camp and buried just beyond the barbed-wire entanglements.

But burying did little good, for we could not dig down very deep in the mud. At night the torrential rains washed the dead out again. They were left to be preyed on by wild dogs and vultures.

All during this time rumours ran wild. Weldon wanted to believe them most. They were crazy rumours of hope, clutched by dying men. Weldon tried hard to make us believe them. Each day he brought us a new one.

'I hear they're going to exchange us. They're going to send us back to America.'

The next day he had another rumour. 'I hear the Americans have made a landing on the island. We'll be saved.

We'll soon be free. The American Army will set us free.'

Still the days dragged away and men died like flies. For some strange reason the Japanese began to care about us. They sent Japanese doctors into the camp. The doctors held their noses as they walked among us, checking on our conditions. At last they notified all the men who were able to walk to appear on the hill near the headquarters buildings, and to bring their belongings.

Most of us had very little personal possessions, but when a man died he was stripped of his clothing by the living and what little gear and possessions he owned were put to further use. We lined up there on the hill, and we heard another lecture by the Japanese officers.

They told us we would be sent to a different camp. Conditions would be better there. We would have more food. We would receive medicine. But we would have to work. There would be no food for the men who did not work.

Somehow I felt that they would keep their word. But I knew that none of us would be able to work unless we had food and medicine first.

They divided us into three groups and said that each group would be sent to a different island. We were lucky, for my friends and I were able to stay together. We were loaded on trucks and driven across the island down to Manila.

It was strange to see Manila again. I had not seen it since the night we left to go to the war on Bataan. Peace had returned to Manila, peace without the menace of war. The American Army was far away. There was a routineness and a normality about the city. There were smiles on the faces of the Filipinos. As we drove through the streets, they held up their hands, unmindful of the Japanese conquerors. They formed a V for victory with their fingers. They smiled, hoping to give us a belief in their loyalty.

There was also defiance in their eyes as they looked at the Japs, and a passive resistance in their actions. I watched them as they passed the Japanese guards, bowing low as they were required to do. The Japanese had become kinder. But it was the kindness of a conqueror, secure in his victory.

We were glad of the change and the increased ration of food we obtained. In Manila they gave us fruit and bananas and more rice than we had had in a long time. Then we were loaded on a little Japanese inter-island steamer. We started off down through the chain of islands. We stopped at Cebu. The city was old and beautiful, and peace had returned here, peace under a new conqueror.

As I looked at the city, at the old walls, I thought how many times the islands had been under the domination of foreign nations. They had been under the Spanish, the Portuguese, the English, the Spanish again, the Americans and now the Japanese. But they liked the Americans best. They showed that in their attitude, in their willingness to fight beside us on Bataan. It was something to feel proud of, and God knows just then we had little.

The boat moved slowly on its way. We were allowed more freedom on the ship, more movement, and the guards laughed and joked with us. There were very few slappings and beatings, and our food was good. When we put into ports they even allowed the Filipinos to throw fruit to us.

When we pulled into Zamboanga I felt Rass grip my arm.

'Look, Sid,' Rass said. 'Aren't they beautiful?'

I followed his eyes out to the Moro *vintas*. There must

have been five hundred of them sailing in the bay. They
were unbelievably beautiful, with their multi-hued sails of
red and white stripes, solid red silk, or blue or brown stripes
running in every direction. Many of them had a gold Moro
crescent in the centre of the sail. The boats were beautifully
carved and they sailed like a toy fleet.

'You know, not many years ago these little boats were
commanded by the fiercest pirates in all the southern
islands,' John said in a voice faintly reminiscent of the classroom. 'They used to lie in wait and row out to a ship. After
a few minutes they had it overpowered and sinking. Then
they took all the cargo, made the crew captives and sold
them for slaves.'

'Remember the song, "Red Sails in the Sunset"?' asked a
strange voice beside me.

I turned and looked. He was a very young boy, not more
than seventeen years of age. He had a wide clear forehead,
big blue eyes, and short-cropped hair. I introduced myself.

'My name's David,' he said, 'but they call me Ohio.
Everybody calls me Ohio. You see, I'm from Ohio and
they say I talk about it too much. That's how I got the nick-
name.'

We both laughed.

'Well, I don't think that makes you a social outcast, just
because you're a Yankee.'

'Aw, listen to Stew,' John threw in. 'He's just an Okie.
Don't pay any attention to that guy. That's the trouble
with these Okies. They don't fall into any classification,
either North or South.'

'Well, at least you're not from Texas,' Weldon said. 'I'm
sick and tired of hearing all about Texas.'

The newcomer gestured toward the sunlit fleet.

'By golly, that would be worth coming out here to see and all,' he said seriously, 'if it weren't for the Japanese.'

We all laughed. From that time we adopted Ohio into our group. He was a great favourite. Everybody liked him, for he was young and innocent in many ways.

At last the boat reached the southern tip of Mindanao and we were taken off at Davao. Here we were loaded on trucks again and driven fifty miles up into the centre of the jungle to a new prison camp in a clearing. The camp was clean, the buildings were good and the roofs, of corrugated iron, were strong and would hold out the weather. Wells were dotted about the camp. We were told it had been used as a penal colony by the Philippine Government before the war.

We hadn't been there long before other prisoners began to arrive from many sections of the islands. We saw men from Corregidor for the first time. They had been captured a month after we were, and I knew how terrible we must look to them. For they were in good health. They still had all of their gear, their clothing and their toilet articles. Enlisted men came through the gates carrying their barracks bags. Officers still had their foot lockers. There were Navy men and Marines among them. Then a few days passed and more men arrived.

These men were from Del Monte on the northern tip of Mindanao. They had been in the Air Corps and they too had received a different treatment. They too had all their gear. The Japanese had not taken their personal possessions. They still had fountain pens and rings. Their rights as prisoners had been respected, and they could no more believe us than we them.

For hours we used to sit around and tell of our horrible experiences, of the Death March and the two months in Camp O'Donnell.

But as we rested, and had more food, and all the water we wanted to bathe in and to drink, we who came from Bataan became stronger and well again. We were divided into details and told that we would have to work. We would have to raise our own food and food for the Japanese. There would be other work details also.

The death rate dropped. Finally the day came when all the men were expected to go out to work. To prevent men from goldbricking, the Japs refused to give a ration of food to the sick. However, in the beginning sick men were not forced to work. Men who could work shared their food with the sick. When they came down with malaria, their friends in turn shared with them.

The work was varied and some of it was interesting. Men were set to ploughing fields. Others were put on details chopping wood, others, to harrowing fields and planting. Some men were taken out to build roads. We had latrines. There was even a detail which tried to protect the camp from malaria by preventing the growth of the larvae.

Soon many of us began to learn the Japanese language. John and I worked hardest at it. But Weldon was not interested. He considered it degrading.

'I wouldn't learn to speak the bastard's language,' he said bitterly. 'I don't want to know how to speak Nip. I can get along without that.' The miner nodded at the Englishman, Hughes, who shared all his opinions.

John and I kept at it, and Rass joined us at times. But as

soon as he had learned enough pidgin English, a half-English, half-Japanese way of speaking, he no longer cared to learn. John and I, however, were more determined every day to speak it well.

'You know, Stew, I believe that if we learn to speak Japanese well, then when we talk to the Nips, they will forget that we are enemies, because we won't talk with an accent.' The grey eyes in his fragile face grew serious. 'Then we will understand them, and they will understand us.'

We worked until we could speak Japanese very well. At last we began to understand them, their strange superstitions, their background and civilization. In the evening after work I met Ohio and we walked together around the compound. His cropped sandy hair reminded me of a school boy's crew cut. He had a child-like exuberance even in the way he walked. When he looked at me with his wide blue eyes I had the feeling that he saw the world with a youthful freshness. His golden vision rubbed off on whomever he was with. I found myself examining the trees with a sense of discovery.

'This fence they have around this compound is odd, isn't it?' I said, looking at the living fenceposts that they had made of kapok.

'The kapok tree is a funny tree,' Ohio mused. I nodded, for I had never seen a grown tree whose trunk you could cut into sections which, replanted, would sprout and grow again.

'I think the Nips put these living fenceposts in,' Ohio said, 'because any other kind of fence posts would rot within a few days in this darn wet ground, and you could push them over with your fingers.'

I nodded.

'Say, Stew,' he said after a moment's thought. 'You know we have something in Ohio that I bet you'd like.'

I smiled. Ohio again.

'In Ohio we have pawpaws. Did you ever taste a pawpaw?' he asked.

I grinned, but his face was serious, so I said, 'Well, no, Ohio, I've never tasted one. What are they like?'

As we walked on he told me about this strange fruit of his native land. I enjoyed walking with him. He was so young. He seemed to be untouched by his surroundings and the horrors of his prison camp experiences. He had been only a boy when his mother allowed him to join the army, and he had never smoked a cigarette, had a drink or slept with a woman. He became every man's kid brother. The other prisoners, hardened by years, looked upon him as something to protect. He became a symbol of their lost youth and their lost innocence. Had I known then what would later happen to him. . . .

When night fell I left him and went to my own hut. My friends were bedding down for the night. As I fell asleep I heard Hughes whispering to Weldon about the steam puddings his mother used to make.

5 Davao Penal Colony, Southern Mindanao: Autumn 1943

I STOOD UP. Placing my hands on my hips I bent backwards to ease the long strain of stooping in the rice paddy. From where I stood I could see Ohio. He was planting rice beside Scroggins. The hot sun glared down on our bare skins. Using the back of my muddy hand I wiped the sweat from my forehead.

A guard yelled and I bent back to my work. Rass and and John were on either side of me, knee deep in the gooey mud, planting the little seedlings in a line, moving gradually backwards.

'That's written in iambic pentameter,' John said. He had just finished reciting a poem. It was natural for him to discuss the poetic technique. In fact, Rass and I always said we were reading John. He started to recite again, but I wasn't listening. I was thinking of Ohio up ahead and of something that had happened the day before.

Ohio and Scroggins sat together on the stump of an old tree inside the compound. Scroggins was a big, surly man, whom few of us liked. He seldom talked to anyone, just sat around with his own thoughts. Most of the others avoided him, for he was rather mean. He was more than six feet tall and wide across the shoulders, and his life as a sailor had given him an ape-like, lumbering gait.

Ohio and Scroggins were laughing and talking, when Jack Lear, one of the men nearby, let out a string of obscene curses.

Scroggins got up from his seat on the stump and walked over to the man. With one swing of his muscular arm he sent the man sprawling flat across the ground.

'I don't like to hear nobody cuss like that around the kid.' He ground the words between his teeth and we stared open-mouthed. Every man knew he meant it.

Then I remembered one evening when we were coming in from a work detail. As we stopped before the gate, the Japanese guards moved in among us to see if we had stolen any food. Ohio had tried to slip in a potato, which he had hidden in his pants leg.

When the Jap guard found it, Johnson, one of the older men, took the blame.

'I gave the kid the potato,' he told the guard in Japanese. 'It was me that stole it.'

Before we marched on inside the compound, Johnson took a terrific beating for the kid.

I wondered why it was that so many men looked upon the boy as they did. I was brought out of my reverie by a Jap guard's screaming, 'Yoshimei! Yoshimei!' 'Rest! All men rest!'

We crawled up out of the rice paddy and sat along the dykes for a ten-minute rest period. John and I sat together. One of the Jap guards was smoking. The prisoners tried to catch his eye for the butt. We all craved tobacco. John and I used our old plan. We sat quietly, appearing not to notice the guard and his cigarette. Because of our indifference, he looked over at us.

'You no smoke?' he asked.

I nodded my head. 'Yes, I smoke.'

'Yes, I smoke too,' John said.

He seemed to appreciate our show of dignity and complete indifference. He reached in his pocket and pulled out a package of cigarettes, then handed a cigarette to each of us. We lit them and smoked a while in silence.

The guard moved over and sat down beside us. He wanted to talk and, as was usual with them, he pulled a picture from his billfold and showed it to us.

I looked at it a moment. It was a picture of a Japanese woman in a kimono. Beside her stood a little girl. She looked like a little doll. I complimented him on them.

'My wife and daughter,' he said with pride.

We chatted with him a little while, trying to keep our Japanese as free from accent as possible. Suddenly he turned to me.

'Are you married?' he asked.

According to our plan and understanding of their way of life, I hesitated a moment.

'No. I was too young when I entered the army, and my father had not yet picked me a suitable bride,' I said seriously. Out of the corner of my eye I could see John grinning. But the Jap guard's eyes lit up.

'Oh, you aristocrat?' he said. 'You not like the other Americans who marry anybody they please?'

'No,' I smiled. 'Just like in your country, I have to wait for my father to pick me a proper bride.'

'My name is Maurii,' he said.

This was the beginning of our association with Maurii. He looked upon John and me as a cut above the average American. Whenever he was our guard, we watched our language. We didn't curse, nor did we beg for cigarettes. He always tried to shift us to the easier sections of the details, where the work was less. He often gave John and me a full cigarette to smoke. Once in a while he slipped us an entire package, which we took inside the camp and split with our other friends, or used to trade for things we needed.

One night as we sat around the camp fire inside the prison compound talking about home and about the things we wanted to do when we got back, one of the boys crawled over and sat down beside John. They began to talk about music. It was Frankie Francini, a boy from Albuquerque, New Mexico.

'You know, I've played the violin all my life,' I overheard him say. 'I think the thing I miss most, even more than food, is my music.'

They talked a long time about it. He said that he had played since he was a child. I watched him talk. Francini had a pinched, serious little face. He was small-boned and frail, and he used over-emotional words typical of his Italian background, while his black eyes sparkled.

'If I had my violin now, I could play songs you'd like, John,' he said. 'I could play and Yeagers could sing.'

I looked across the fire. Yeagers was singing now. He was a tall boy, also from New Mexico, and he sang mainly western songs, which were popular with the whole group. I listened for a moment to his song.

'Oh, I was born in Renfrow Valley,' he sang in a clear tenor voice.

I could see Francini's fingers moving almost as though they held a violin.

The next morning Rassmussen and I were put on a detail in which we had to clear out one of the old warehouses they planned to use for rice storage. Maurii was one of our guards. After we had worked for some time we had our rest period. We sat down inside the old building for a little while. Looking up, my eyes fell on an old violin hanging near the rafters.

I punched Rass. 'Look! A violin.'

'Wouldn't it be wonderful,' he said, brushing his hair back off his forehead, 'if we could get that violin for Francini? He could play for us in the evenings.'

'Oh, I don't know, Rass. I doubt if the strings are any good. It's probably been hanging there a long time and they're all either missing or broken.'

But as our work wore on I couldn't get the thought out of my mind. Sometime later I noticed Rass had worked himself over near the wall. He was looking at the violin. He turned around and yelled at me.

'Stew, three of the strings are here. They're all right. There's only one that's gone.'

I worked my way over near him.

'Well, Rass, I don't know anything about music myself. I don't know how to play a violin. I don't know if you could play it with three strings.'

'I don't know either,' he said. 'I don't see how in the world we could get it anyway.'

Maurii was standing near the door. I turned to Rass.

'Let me try it on old Maurii. I've always been able to get a few things out of him. There might be just the chance he'd let us have it.'

During the next rest period I made my way over to him and sat down close by. I talked to him a little bit about Japan and about his home, about what he wanted to do when he got out of the army. Then I looked up at the wall where the violin hung.

'Maurii,' I said, 'could I have the violin there on the wall?'

He followed my gaze a minute. 'You play music?' he said.

'No, but I have a friend in the prison camp who plays very well,. and it doesn't look like it belongs to anyone. Could I have it?' I tried to keep the eagerness out of my voice.

'It isn't mine to give.' His voice was flat. 'But you wait. I will find out.'

When our rest period was over and we went back to work, I kept watching him. But nothing was said and finally we were led back to the prison camp in the evening.

'Well, it looks like we don't get it,' I said to Rass when the log gates were closed behind us. 'I don't know when we'll get a chance to work over there again. If we did it's too big to try and steal.'

'No,' Rass said. 'We'd never be able to smuggle it back inside the prison camp.'

We washed ourselves and drew our ration of rice for the evening meal. Then one of the prisoners came to me.

'Old Maurii is down by the gate. He has something for you. He wants you to come down there.'

Quickly I made my way to the gate. I found him waiting and under his arm was the old violin.

'I brought you this, *tamadachi*.' His white teeth showed in a grin.

I took it, held it in my hands a minute before looking up at him, wanting him to see my thanks.

'*Origato haitai san*,' I thanked him.

He nodded. Without speaking he turned and walked out of the gates and closed them behind him. I ran back as fast as I could to where my friends were sitting around the camp fire.

'Francini!' I yelled. 'I've got it! I've got it!' The prisoners gathered around me and I showed them the violin. 'I don't know anything about a violin, Frankie,' I said, 'but this has got three strings.'

He was breathless as he took the violin, like a hungry man reaching for food. He ran his hands softly across the old wood. When I looked at his face there were tears in his eyes.

'The bow is a good one,' he said. 'I can play on just three strings. I'll have to transpose, of course, and it won't be quite as good—oh, wait!'

His eyes had fallen on something down inside the violin. It looked like a small piece of white cloth.

'Wait a minute.' Taking a twig, he worked it down through the little hole and pulled out the cloth. It had been soaked in oil, and inside was wrapped the G string. He opened it up, stretching it slowly.

'Oh, it's all here. It's not broken,' he cried. He stretched it on the violin and then slowly tuned it. We sat down around the fire and waited.

Suddenly he began to play. The music drifted slowly and then rose until it seemed to colour the air with our dreams. No great concert artist ever played before a more appreciative audience. And no one ever played with more heart and soul than Francini played at that moment.

I closed my eyes and imagined myself at home listening to music in some great hall. Francini played the waltzes from Gounod's *Faust*. When I opened my eyes I saw that there were tears pouring down John's cheeks. Never had I heard anything so beautiful.

Pretty soon Yeagers came over and stood by him, and Francini played, 'I Dreamt I Dwelt in Marble Halls'. Yeagers began to sing. His clear tenor voice blended with the violin, rang across the camp. I don't know if music in Heaven is like that, but I do know we had missed it from our lives. At home, in America, there is music in the heart of everything, in the laughter of children playing, in the slap of tires on wet pavement, in the juke-box in the corner drug store. Hearing it again, we forgot we were prisoners in a lonely camp in the centre of the Mindanao jungles. We were home again listening to music that made a luxury of living.

But things did not always go so well. One evening as I came in from work I sensed a gloom that hung low over the entire camp. There was no laughter and cheering as the men ran with their buckets to the wells to wash. There was nothing but a strange desolate stillness. The men walked about silently.

As I walked into our hut, John met me at the door.

'They killed Ohio,' he said quietly.

'Killed Ohio!' I screamed.

'Yes, killed him. He was caught stealing some potatoes on the *camote* detail. He was beaten to death this evening.'

The battered body was brought inside the camp later and carried over beside the camp fire. The prisoners stood around helpless. Too late. Wanting to do something for the boy who had given them so much. But he was gone and there was no man with a dry eye.

We sat around the camp fire, no man talking, each with his own thoughts, remembering the kid's smiles, his silly chatter, how he had depended upon us. Because of that dependence he had made better men of us all.

As we sat there in silence, suddenly Yeagers stood up. Then he began to sing and his voice floated out across the camp over our heads and into our hearts. He sang:

> 'Beautiful Ohio in dreams again I see
> Visions of what used to be. . . .'

I had always thought that the song was of a river, but now it would always be for me a song about a boy seventeen years old who came from Ohio. Just a kid, but he had given us back things that the Japanese had tried to take away.

6 Davao Penal Colony, Davao, Mindanao: December 1943

THE JAPANESE bugle blew each morning when it was still dark, echoing a mournful Oriental note over the jungle and the camp. We rolled out of our makeshift beds of old burlap sacks on the damp dirt floor, and ran through the darkness to the mess hall. In the east the sky turned a bluish green. We drew our ration of steaming rice and sat down on the ground to eat. One morning Weldon yawned and stretched like a powerful cat, and then turned to Hughes.

'What detail are you on today, Limey?'

'I've got to make baskets today.' His nose inhaler had long since disappeared and he had developed the habit of pulling on his nose while he talked. 'I'm not very tidy at it though.'

He had been put on that detail because he had been sick for a week with malaria. He was still white and weak, but he could do some work and draw a food ration.

'What are you on, Sid?' Rass asked me.

'I have to plough today,' I said wearily.

'I'll bet you guys can't guess what I have to do today,' Weldon's laughter boomed.

'No, what?' asked John.

'Well, you know there aren't any bees down here.'

'Yeah, what has that got to do with it?' I asked impatiently.

'Well, you see, without bees things don't pollinate themselves. So I've got to go with a detail of men to the squash patch.' He grinned. 'We've got to go around and pick the male blossoms off the pumpkin vines and pollinate the female blossoms.'

'Closest thing to sex you've had in a long time, I'll bet,' said John. We all laughed, and the bell rang and we went to line up with our work details.

Unfortunately I drew old Jim, one of the slowest carabaos in the whole group. The huge black water buffalo smelled like stagnant water, and he was caked with mud. For relief from the heat and the flies, when he is not being worked, the carabao immerses his entire body in mud wallows. He lies for hours with only his huge head protruding and the long thick horns curving behind. The carabao are slow and stoic like oxen. They move at a snail's pace, their sleepy brown eyes half closed, and constantly chew their cud.

I began to plough the rice paddy, churning up the gooey mud. Suddenly the animal stopped dead still. I slapped the reins across his back, but he only shook his lazy head and just stood there. I went around and began to pull him by the horns, but he would not move. I tried kicking and swearing, but Jim was baulkier than any mule I had ever seen. Finally one of the Jap guards came over.

'Why you no work?' he said, a dim threat edging his voice.

I pointed at the animal helplessly. He slapped my face.

'You work,' he demanded. '*Hosame quicko!*'

Again I began to beat on the animal and still it would

not go. The disgusted contempt of the Nip was something outrageous.

'Me, I show you,' he grunted. He took the reins in his own hands and tried beating the animal. But apparently to a carabao even a Jap beating was a trifle in the wind. Old Jim merely snorted and stood his ground. Finally, looking very serious, the Jap guard walked to the back of the animal and unhitched his bayonet.

'I fix him,' he announced. 'I fix him so with all the other carabao he lose face.' With one quick swing he whacked old Jim's thick tail clear off.

Maybe old Jim didn't realize it was face he was losing, but of dire loss there was no doubt in his mind. With a terrific bellow he broke into a run. I flew along behind, clinging to the handles of the plough. The carabao hurdled one of the small dykes, pulling the plough through it. The water rushed through the opening as the animal headed across another paddy and through another dyke and on into the next paddy before I could stop it. By now all of the Jap sentries were screaming and the men were holding their sides and roaring with laughter.

It took us until noon to repair the dykes. The guards stood by, angry and serious and a little bewildered by the Americans, who were weak from laughter. We were given our issue of rice and allowed to rest for an hour. We sat around on the banks of the other paddies with our feet dangling in the muddy water. A Jap truck drove by on the road, choking. Suddenly, it stopped.

The Jap soldier jumped out and ran around to the front of the engine and beat on it with his fists. Then he jumped back inside the cab and tried to start it again. It wouldn't go. He jumped out again and grabbed a stick and began to hit the engine. We were afraid to laugh loud, knowing that he would take out his anger on us. I looked the other way, gritting my teeth for fear of laughing.

The action was typical of the Japanese national character. Only since he had come into the army had the average soldier learned how to drive trucks. He had learned precious little even then. As far as he was concerned, there was a little devil that sat just under the hood. It wouldn't make the truck go unless it wanted to, and often it just didn't.

I could understand, watching that screaming Nip, why he hated the Americans. The little devil in the truck seemed to know the Americans, for almost any American could lift up the hood, talk to the little devil for a while, and the truck would go roaring down the road. The puzzled Jap hated us for this mystery that he thought was so superior. But he acknowledged it in his own quaint way. If one of the Americans was unable to fix the car, he would scream, 'Sabotage me!' and beat the American unmercifully.

As I watched now, one of the Americans walked forward and in a few minutes had the engine going. The Jap gave him a black scowl as a reward, jumped inside the truck and went roaring down the road in a cloud of dust. Silently I hoped he'd break his neck on the next turn.

As the dust settled I looked at the impenetrable jungle that surrounded us, and remembered idly how often we had thought of escape.

That was before the Japs had divided the entire camp into groups of ten men. If one took off, the nine remaining would be taken out and shot. Now, out of loyalty to each other, we did not try to escape even when we had the opportunity. Yet, I wondered, thinking about the times we had planned an escape, how we would have penetrated that jungle.

Its dense growth was a wild tangled mass of vines that swung down and grabbed you, encircling your body, a strange place of deep swamps and heavy growth never before crossed by a white man. It was a wall of nature stronger than any the Japanese could have built themselves.

Loyalty to our friends prevented us from trying to escape, and a man needed friends to survive in prison camp. They worked beside him and shared their food when he was sick. They bathed him when he was burning up with fever. They talked to him when his spirits were low and some times saved his life. His friends would die if he escaped. So we waited for the time when we would be free.

In the prison compound that night I sat with my friends around the camp fire in the centre of the compound. John talked in his low voice, turning the album pages of his amazing memory. He could quote whole pages of Shakespeare, not a half-dozen lines wrong, I am sure even today. Since we had no books to read we all concentrated and dug up from memory poems we used to love and songs we liked. It was astonishing how much we remembered.

We talked, too, of home until each man knew every member of the other man's family almost as well as he knew his own. Rassmussen told with amusement stories of his staid, stiff-backed church background. One was about his grandfather, an elder in the church, who had prayed so hard for rain that, when he left the church, it rained so hard that his team of horses drowned.

We all told jokes from our childhood, and we sang songs,

sitting around the camp fire. Hughes told us about his life in England, and quoted poems by Rupert Brooke and William Butler Yeats. Weldon told about his life in the coal mines. I talked about the red clay hills I loved in Oklahoma.

As I looked at their faces, lit by the light of the camp fire, I could see how thin and drawn they had become with the months and years in prison. I thought of the character within each man. Rassmussen, with his firm belief in God, was never too tired to help with a wounded or sick man. He was always willing to share what little he had. Then I looked at John, who was always so kind and sympathetic. He was the best listener in the crowd, and everyone liked to talk to him.

Hughes was the weak one among us. We understood him too well. Weldon always protected him. Their bond of friendship never ceased to amaze me. Hughes still wore his little moustache. I remembered when his weakness nearly cost us all our lives. He had taken our little cache of quinine, our precious little store of five grain tablets. He had taken them without asking and traded them for something he wanted. And Weldon had protected him, desperate as the situation was.

The Japanese occasionally issued a certain amount of quinine, which was divided up among the men. It was never enough, and we always tried to keep at least sixty tablets on hand for fear one man's fever might get high. There was no easy way to save the men except with a little quinine to break the fever—there was never enough to cure it. But if you could break the fever, you could hold it off until another attack came.

Once, returning from the evening's work, I found my

friends sitting on the floor of the grass hut, their eyes wide
with fear.

'Someone has stolen our quinine,' Weldon snarled.

I remember the shock of it. Where could we get more?
Already John was burning up with fever.

'Hughes,' Rass's voice was flat, hard. 'Tell them what
happened to the quinine.'

'Why—I don't know—what happened,' Hughes said falter-
ingly, pulling nervously at his nose.

'Hughes, tell them what happened to the quinine,' Rass
repeated. All our eyes turned to Hughes.

'Do you know what happened to that quinine?' Weldon
said.

Hughes looked down at the ground.

'Yes. I—I traded it.'

'You traded it!' we screamed. What in the world was so
valuable that he would trade quinine—quinine, a matter
of life and death—for it? Then we noticed he was wearing
a jacket. It was the first time we had seen it. We all knew
that he had traded our quinine for a jacket. Suddenly I
hated him. But Weldon spoke up quickly in his defence.

'All right, you guys, take it easy. What's done is done,'
the big miner said patiently. 'Hughes couldn't help it. He
just didn't think.'

'Didn't think—hell!' I screamed. 'Anybody's got more
sense than that.'

But John, lying on the floor, his face flushed with fever,
only shook his head. 'There's nothing in this world big
enough, or bad enough to make us quarrel,' he said. 'Or
hate each other. Not after what we've gone through, we
mustn't.'

Without answering, Rass and I turned our backs on them and walked out of the building. We walked up and down, thinking. What could we do? We had to get quinine for John. He had to have it. When we calmed down we went back and held our little council of war.

'I'll tell you what we'll have to do,' Rass said at last. 'We'll just have to go without food for the next two days. None of us will eat. We'll draw our rations, and we'll go around to the other men and trade our food for a quinine tablet apiece. But we've got to borrow some of these in advance, because John has to have quinine tonight.'

For two days we went without food. Hughes drew his ration and gave half of it to John. We made him eat the other half of it himself. We stood there making him eat it in front of us, wanting him to feel small. But somehow Weldon's faith and friendship made us feel small ourselves.

Weldon understood Hughes. Hughes had had an easy life. He had come from a wealthy family. He had never worked. He had never had to sacrifice. Weldon, who had had to work from the time he was a young boy, who had never had things, who had never had an education, could understand Hughes and could forgive him. In the end we all forgave him.

During the first days of December 1943, the men began to avoid talk of home. I could not bear to talk of home or even think of it. Christmas was coming and Christmas in a prison camp is cruel. It hurts when you think of home at Christmas. A man's thoughts and dreams of his family torture him even more when he is hungry and tired and feels deserted by his homeland.

The rations were getting slimmer every day and the

attitude of the Japanese was more suspicious and mean. One day the work did not go as they thought it should. They gave us no rest and we laboured until long after the sun had gone down and it had begun to rain, a cold tropical rain. In our sick, half-starved condition the cold was much worse. It grew darker. Still we went on planting the rice in the paddies. The Japs' screams of irritation echoed around us, shattering the silence in the jungle.

It was almost midnight before they allowed us to come out of the paddies and line up in four columns. We had nine miles to walk back to the camp. As we started back, sloshing with our bare feet in the mud of the road and with the cold rain falling on our bare backs, the men were grimly silent.

We'll never see home again, I was thinking. It looks like we'll never see it. We are so hungry. We're all sick. We're tired and it's nearly Christmas. The war will never end—never end. Very softly, before we had gone a mile, someone began to hum, then sing. Gradually it was taken up by the rest of us. The Japanese sentries ran in among us, beating us on the backs, kicking us on the shins and screaming. But we would not stop. The jungle rang with our singing all the long, black miles back to camp. And the song we sang was 'God Bless America'.

Only when the prison gates were thrown back and we entered the compound did the voices stop. But when we went to our little huts and lay down for the night, each man felt stronger. I was proud of my friends, proud of the unbeaten spirit of those who were with me. Nothing the Japanese could do would shake our faith in ourselves and our land.

When the night before Christmas came, few of us slept. I lay there all night, my eyes open, trying not to think of home. But always the picture of my mother and father and my family, and the tree bright with its lights, and the Christmas carols kept crowding into my mind.

It was dark and no one could see the tears that flooded my eyes. I could cry without shame. But as the first light of the tropical morning struck the sky we were awakened by the most glorious choir we had ever heard in our lives. The voices rang out across the camp, singing with heart and soul, 'Joy to the World, the Lord Has Come'. Surprised, we rolled out of our bunks and ran outside.

There was a group of about two hundred prisoners, bare-footed, and dressed in rags, their faces thin, many with beards, singing to us with all their hearts, wishing us a Merry Christmas. For God had come down to earth to save men, and it was Christmas, Christmas in a prison camp.

When they finished singing I asked one of the men how it had come about. Major Pritchard had begged permission of the Japanese for the detail to sing while they worked. He had taught them the Christmas carols and trained them. As they worked side by side in the fields the men separated themselves according to their tone parts. They practised so that they could give us these songs for Christmas.

But Christmas passed and the days dragged by. Weeks passed. Months passed. Spring came again, approaching the summer of 1944. Rumours ran thick and fast. The American Army was getting close. We heard they were in the Celebes. There was no way to verify this, but some of the men had overheard the Japanese guards talking.

The guards were getting meaner all the time, and their

flare-ups of anger were more frequent. They watched the skies, and they built emplacements for their own protection around the edges of the camp. We knew the Americans must be getting close.

7 *Summer* 1944

ONE AFTERNOON in May, while the sun still shone high in the sky, we were called out of the fields. All the prisoners were ordered back to the main prison camp.

I could see the men converging toward the prison compound from all directions. It was early in the afternoon and I wondered why we were being sent back. Had someone escaped? But the guards did not seem serious or frightened. They even laughed and joked as they walked along beside us without any particular hurry.

Later in the afternoon we were ordered out in front of the barracks and into a long line. We were counted and divided into groups. Then I saw the Japanese doctor, Yashamura, walking slowly down the line.

When he came to my group he looked at me a long time. I caught my breath as he smiled and nodded for me to stand to the side. I walked over and stood with the rapidly enlarging circle of men who had been chosen. What were they going to do with us? But I saw that all the men around me were healthier and stronger than the men he had not chosen.

When an hour had passed the Japanese doctor completed his examination. He ordered the other men back to their huts. Then one of the Japanese interpreters stood before the group of those who had been chosen.

'You must get your things ready. You are leaving,' he said. 'We are sending you to La Sang.'

'Where is La Sang?' I asked one of the men standing near me.

'Oh, it's a little town about halfway between here and Davao,' he said, low and hopeless like the sound of the wind blowing across dry prairie grass.

I looked back at the Japanese interpreter, but I didn't listen to his words. Suddenly I felt lonely and a little afraid. I was the only one of my group of friends who had been picked. Weldon was sick with malaria. Rass for some reason had been overlooked. Hughes didn't look well, and John had not been strong for some time and had continued to lose weight. There was some strange sickness about him that none of us had been able to understand. He ran a temperature every afternoon.

I hated to be separated from my friends. We had been together for so long now that our lives were interdependent. As soon as we were dismissed I walked back into the hut. I rolled up my little stock of belongings and then I looked over at my friends without speaking. They knew how I hated to leave them. I could see in their eyes how they hated to see me go. Rass walked over and laid his hand on my shoulder. His hand closed, gripping me tight.

'Gosh, fellow,' he said, 'I hate to think of you not being with us. But maybe you're going to a better place. Maybe it'll be all right there. They only picked the strongest. It'll probably be a good work detail.'

'Yeah, it'll be a good deal,' Weldon said gruffly.

They seemed intent on making me feel that I was privileged, that I was getting something they weren't. They wanted me to feel better, and I smiled.

'Yes, it'll probably be a good deal. I'm kinda glad to go.'

But I wasn't, and we had been together too long for me to sell them any act. They knew I wanted to stay with them. Finally I turned my back on them and walked out of the hut. They didn't follow me. They didn't want to see me leave and I couldn't stand to look back at them.

As the trucks pulled away from the compound and down the jungle roads that wound through the vast fields of abaca, I knew how close the Allied Army must be. Everywhere I could see trenches and gun emplacements. The Japanese were preparing for the war that was coming back.

When we arrived at La Sang there were barracks for us, but they were not as good as the ones we had left. These were flimsy structures of bamboo poles and grass roofs with woven swali sides. But there was plenty of room in the camp, for there were only six hundred of us on the detail.

It was early in the evening. They had taken some of the Americans ahead and they had huge caldrons of steaming rice ready for us. Mixed in the rice were large pieces of white fish. It was the largest ration we had received in a long time and it raised our spirits. We began to laugh and talk with each other, for we were all lonesome for our friends.

'Yes, it does look like things are going to be better here,' I said to one of the men.

He nodded with his mouth full of rice.

The next morning the Japanese interpreter lined us up in columns of four again. He stood before us and told us what we were to do. We were going to build an airstrip.

I could feel the indignation rising in me. An airfield for Japanese planes to take off and land on. Japanese planes that would go out and fight American soldiers. I was an American being forced to build an airfield that would be used in the war against America. A war that would kill other Americans. All around me the prisoners were muttering sullenly. I could hear their cursing. I knew they too were hot with resentment.

We were marched out of the camp. We straggled along in columns of four for a distance of about three and a half miles to the place that we were supposed to work. They lined us up again and the Japanese guards divided us into separate sections. Each section was then led forward. Some were given shovels. Another section was given picks, another, wheelbarrows and various other implements. Some men were to work down in the coral pits. Others were to work on the runway smashing the coral rocks into a powdered white dust. Some were to dig, while others carried the dirt away in the wheelbarrows.

We went to work with animosity and resentment, knowing what we were doing and hating the Japs for making us do it. It was dishonourable. Every time I raised my pick and sent it slamming into the ground, I felt that I was helping to kill Americans, other Americans.

At noon we were lined up again. The Japanese interpreter walked back and forth in front of us, gripping his hands until they were white. Occasionally I would hear him snap his knuckles before he began to talk in his clipped, clear English.

'We must build this airfield within six weeks,' he said.

'You will have to work very hard and very quickly. You
will be treated well. We are going to bring issues of tobacco
for every man. You will receive more food, but you must
work hard, very hard. If you are lazy you will be punished.'

When he finished we were given our issue of rice. It was
almost twice as much as we had received at the old camp,
but somehow, hungry as I was, the food seemed to choke
in my throat. I hated it. I felt that it was a reward for
helping the Japanese in a war against America.

That evening we were led back to camp, a group of sullen
and silent men. When the log gates were flung back and
we marched inside, we received our evening ration of rice
and a large piece of white tuna fish. We walked back inside
our huts and sat down to eat. But a sense of gloom and
despondency hung over the entire group of prisoners. No one
talked.

I sat there on the floor of the hut, wondering about my
two brothers. Were they in the army? Would the Japanese
planes that took off from this airfield I was building be
able to bomb and kill my brothers? I looked up from my
meal of rice and fish. The men sat in silent rows along the
walls of the hut. There were a hundred men in each of the
six buildings. I knew that in the other buildings the same
silence, the same resentment, the same despondency existed
as here.

That night when I tried to sleep I lay for a while with
my eyes open, staring at the tiny flickers of light that came
through the grass roof. Suddenly I heard the men whispering
and talking. One of the prisoners asked us to congregate
near the front of the building. Slowly I got up and joined
the others.

'The officers over in building No. 1 are getting up a plan to do something about the work we're doing,' one man whispered so that the group could hear. 'They want each hut to send two men that will represent the rest of us to go and talk with them about what we plan to do.'

'Stew, why don't you represent us?' they said. 'You talk better than most of us, and you got a pretty good education. Whatever you say, the rest of us will stand behind you.'

'Why don't you represent us?' others urged.

I nodded. 'Okay, I'll go.'

They also picked Jackson and the two of us slipped out into the dark. We made our way slowly across the compound toward the first shack. Men from the other shacks were already there. They huddled around a candle, their faces hard and their eyes intense in the flickering light.

'We represent shack No. 3,' I told them.

They made room for us to sit down on the ground with them.

One man was talking and gesturing with his hands. He was an older man, well-built, with determined brown eyes and a strong jaw.

'I was an engineer before the war,' he said. 'Some of you men know me, some of you don't, but my name is Major Kelly. I worked for an oil company in China. I used to wonder, as I watched the Chinese, how they could work so hard and apparently accomplish nothing.'

He talked slowly and we all tried to concentrate on what he said.

'The Chinese have no labour unions,' he went on, 'but they have a way of making a company hire more men.

They work hard, but they don't accomplish anything. It takes terrific teamwork to give the appearance of labouring and still not really accomplish anything. I found that out one time when I saw six men lift a log.

'I watched them for a moment as they strained and grunted trying to pick it up. Then they motioned for two other men to come over and help them. The eight men picked up the log and struggled off with it. As I watched the Chinese walk away with it I went over to the pile of logs and reached down. I picked one up with my hand. They were balsa wood, light as feathers. I understood then how the Chinese get the Americans and the English to hire more men.'

We all huddled a little closer around the candlelight.

'Now here's my plan,' he said seriously. 'I want each one of you to go back to your huts and explain to the men what we want to do. We're going to work. We're going to work hard, and it's going to take more co-operation and teamwork than they realize to convince the Japanese that we are working. Every man when he is using a pick must raise it above his head and try to hit the hole that he made the last time. Play a game of trying not to get any work accomplished, yet work all the time.'

Then he cautioned us again, 'It won't be easy. It sounds easy, but there is something much harder about work that is futile. The men mustn't get lazy. They must keep up appearances.'

When the council was finished we crawled back out into the dark and made our way to our hut. The men were still awake, waiting. We told them the plan, explaining how it was to work. Every one of them must labour harder than he had before to give the impression of working. Still we must not accomplish anything.

That night as I went to sleep I wondered if it would succeed. I prayed that it would. The Japanese were so determined that the airfield should be finished in six weeks. Would the men co-operate? Could they put it over?

When the sun came up the next morning the men looked happier again. There were smiles on their faces as we were led out to work. We walked along and some of the men laughed and kidded each other. Some whistled. Some sang. They had gotten confidence in themselves again. Each group was given picks and shovels and wheelbarrows, and we started to work. We worked awfully hard, but somehow there was pleasure in it and a certain amount of fun.

I was on a shovel on this day. I would move a little pile of dirt to one place, and then very intently and seriously move it a few feet away. When one of the wheelbarrows came by, the man stopped for a moment and filled the wheelbarrow very high, very heavy. The Jap guard grinned with approval as the man on the wheelbarrow started off. The barrow man wound his way in among the working Americans. Suddenly he slipped, as soon as he was out of sight of the guard. Accidentally the wheelbarrow turned over and spilled upon the ground.

Very seriously one of the men brought his shovel over. Again he picked up the dirt and filled the wheelbarrow.

Men on the picks would raise them high above their head, then slam a hole into the ground. Then they played the game of seeing how many times they could hit that hole with the sharp end of the pick.

At the end of the day only one foot had been made on the runway. Yet the Japs congratulated us, commenting on how well we were working, and promised to give us more tobacco and a larger portion of rice. We were fed better when we got back to the camp than we had been in a long time.

Again we had a council meeting. When I returned to my hut after the meeting I cautioned the men on how important it was that we keep up the teamwork. We had to keep the Japanese happy, but we still must not accomplish anything. We had to work harder than we had ever worked before. The men lay down to sleep each night exhausted, for work is much harder when nothing is accomplished.

After four weeks had dragged by and only a few yards of the runway had been completed, the Japs doubled the guard on the detail. With perplexed looks on their faces, the Japanese engineers ran in among us, watching us closely. Yet none of the men was beaten for not working. They could see with their own eyes that we were working very hard. Yet nothing was being done, nothing was accomplished.

As I looked at their puzzled faces I gritted my teeth to keep from bursting into laughter. I had become so skilled I could hit the same hole with my pick ten times running without even breaking the edges.

Late in the afternoon I began to feel a cold chill. My body was shaking all over. I knew I was having malaria again. I felt hot and sick and my blood was pounding in my temples. I was dizzy. Suddenly I felt that I could stand no longer.

'I feel like I'm going to pass out,' I said to one of the men standing near me.

He reached over and laid his hand against my head.

'You're hot as an iron stove,' he said. 'You'd better go over and ask the Jap for permission to lie down.'

I laid my pick down on the ground and walked over to the Japanese guard.

'*Bioki, haitai san. Tien bioke,*' I said. 'Malaria.' I pointed at my head.

He looked at me keenly, squinting his eyes. It must have been apparent even to him that I was burning up with fever, for he motioned me to go over and lie down on the ground.

As I lay there I felt that my blood was boiling inside, boiling and exploding inside my body. Then suddenly I felt cold, terribly cold, as though I was freezing. I lay there shivering, shaking from head to foot, my teeth chattering. Then the fever came back again, and I gasped for breath. My head swam, my sight was blurry, my eyes watered. I lost consciousness.

When I came to, a slow tropical rain was falling, and the Japanese were blowing whistles, calling the men out of the work. Jackson came over to me and looked down. Then he knelt on one knee and felt my head.

'How you doing, fellow?' he said. 'You look pretty bad.'

The blood was pounding in my ears, and his voice sounded far away.

'We're starting back to the camp,' he said. 'Come on, I'll help you get to your feet.'

He ran his hand in around my shoulder, and I struggled

to my feet. He put one of my arms over his shoulder and called to another man to help him. They half-carried me the three-and-a-half miles back to the prison compound. I had no sense of what was going on around me, only a terrible fatigue and a pain each time I tried to breathe. I had a horrible pain in my back and in my lungs. I gritted my teeth and sucked the air in slowly. It hurt too bad if I let my lungs fill quickly.

Jackson spent the night bathing me with cold water and rubbing my arms and legs. I bit my tongue, stifling the scream that rose to my throat each time I tried to take a breath. My head pounded with fever.

Late in the night I came to. Through the blur, I heard a voice. It sounded hazy and far away. Then I recognized it. It was one of the American doctors who worked with us.

'He's got pneumonia,' I heard the doctor say.

The voice sounded far away to me.

'Is there anything we can do for him, doctor?'

I recognized Jackson's voice.

'I'm afraid not,' the doctor said. 'I'll try to get the Japs to give me something tomorrow, a little medicine or something. But there's nothing we can do if they don't. Just try to watch him. Otherwise I'm afraid he's a goner.'

I lapsed into unconsciousness again, but I could still hear that voice, echoing, like a call in an empty house. *I'm afraid he's a goner, I'm afraid he's a goner, I'm afraid he's a goner.*

Suddenly I wanted to fight. I had to fight. I had to live.

The next day passed and I lay in a daze, not knowing what went on around me. It must have been late in the night when I came to again, for I could hear the heavy snores of the men around me, sleeping exhaustedly. I knew I was groaning and crying. It hurt to breathe. Every wisp of air that entered my lungs was like the stab of a thousand knives in my back. I felt sure I would die, and I couldn't stifle the screams of pain. I heard the men stirring beside me, muttering in their sleep. They were tired. I felt selfish because I had to scream and groan with pain. Suddenly I knew I couldn't stay there. I couldn't lie there and keep them all awake.

I brought myself to my knees and started crawling out of the hut into the open compound. I reached a tall acacia tree and pulled myself over and propped myself up flat against the trunk. It was easier to breathe in a sitting position. I lay there for a little while, crying, feeling the hot tears running down my cheeks. I continued to cry until I lost consciousness.

When I came to it was early in the evening. Someone was bathing my body with cool water.

'How you doin', fella?'

I heard the voice and it sounded clear, more distinct than it had been before.

'You've been out of your head for days,' Jackson said. 'We've had a hellova time trying to take care of you. I thought sure you was a goner. Then one night the doctor said you passed the crisis.'

I lay back, exhausted, and fell asleep.

The fever passed away, but for two weeks I lay there on the hard ground. The men were good to me. They shared their food with me, sat beside me in the evenings and talked about the work. Laughing at the huge joke and the puzzle and disappointment on the faces of the Japanese. I was proud of them, proud of the tremendous co-operation and teamwork that they were using to defeat our enemies.

But I was so weak I was still not able to work. I still had to crawl. When I tried to bring myself to my feet I was so dizzy that I would faint and had to grab something to keep from falling. One afternoon one of the prisoners came in. He walked over and sat beside me. There was a smile on his face.

'I brought you something,' he said. 'There's a Jap guard out there who says he knows you real well and he gave me something to give you.'

He reached down inside his shirt and pulled out two hard-boiled eggs.

Good old Maurii, I thought. I wanted to give the boy one of the eggs. Without saying a word I handed him an egg.

He laughed. 'No, you keep it,' he said. 'There's a lot of nourishment in those eggs. If you eat 'em you'll get well. The guard said he was going to bring me something like that for you every day. We have to be very careful, you know. The other Japs would raise hell if they found out about it. They'd beat him up for doin' it.'

I smiled and nodded my head. But I waited until he was gone to eat the eggs. I knew it would only make him hungry to see me eat them in front of him. Each day Maurii would send in two, sometimes three eggs, and I felt my strength returning.

One afternoon Doctor Yashamura, the Japanese medical

man, made an inspection of the camp. When he stopped
before me, lying there on the ground of the shack, he bent
down and felt my pulse and examined me.

'I'm going to send you back to the main camp,' he said.
'You are not well enough to work. I'm going to send you
back this evening.'

He smiled and I nodded my head. It would be good to
see my old friends again.

That evening, when the men came in from work, they
helped me to get my things together. Two of them carried
me out and lifted me on to the bed of the truck. There were
three other men beside myself who were sick and were
being sent back to the main camp. The men cheered as the
truck pulled out of the yard. I looked back on them as they
grew small in the distance. Soon the camp disappeared
from sight.

I never saw those men again. I found later that they were
brutally murdered by the Japanese. All were killed, except
for a very few that escaped into the jungle.

The truck bumped along over the winding coral road.

8 *August—October* 1944

THE SUMMER wore on and my strength returned. I was able to go out and work again in the fields. But there was one dark spot in our lives and that was John's strange illness. He was weak and losing more weight all the time.

We tried to spare him. Rass and I put him between us when we went out to work and he crawled beside us in the fields while we were weeding. We could reach across, Rass and I, and pull the weeds for him, doing his share of the work because he was so terribly weak. But we didn't talk about his illness to him. We only watched him and hoped that he would become stronger.

Sunday afternoons were given over to the prisoners to use as they pleased. We did not have to go out to work, and the men spent their time washing their clothes or lounging about in the sun. Few men had the energy for athletic sports of any kind.

One Sunday afternoon was broken by the news that we would be allowed to send word home. The Japanese interpreter entered the camp carrying a stack of yellow postcards. They were distributed and there was a blank line in the centre of the card which each man could fill out with a ten-word message.

My friends and I took our cards and retreated into the hut. We sat there wondering what we could say in ten words.

'I wonder if this means that we will soon be able to get letters from home, too,' Hughes said, pulling on his nose.

'The thing that worries me most,' John added seriously, 'is that if the Japs can send our cards back, maybe the war is not going the way we thought it was. Maybe the Americans won't be here as soon as we expect them.'

'Shut up,' Weldon grunted. 'Don't you think the rest of us feel that way too, without you putting it into words where we have to look at it and think about it even stronger?'

I went outside and sat down on a stump. I took the little pencil that they had given us and figured out my message, trying it many, many ways. Ten words was so inadequate. At last I took the pencil and scribbled:

'Am happy and well and I think always of you.'

I signed it and walked over to the headquarters building and turned my card in.

That night, lying on the ground waiting for sleep to come, I could hear the snores of the men around me. The moon was making a play of light across the yard. I heard the crying of owls in the distance and the various jungle sounds. Every so often I heard the crunching step of the Jap guard just beyond the fence. I couldn't get out of my mind the little ten-word message I had sent. There was so little I could tell them.

I began to pretend that I was writing a letter home. Lying there I tried to think how I would compose a letter to my mother and father back in the States, back in Oklahoma. They would want to know how we lived, what things were

like. I wouldn't tell them the things that were really bad.
I would try to describe our life here, tell them that the men
were fighting every day to keep up their strength and hope.
I started the letter in my mind, muttering the words to myself.

'Our life here as prisoners is a life of long, seemingly endless waiting and hoping.'

Yes, that was the way I would start the letter. Then I went
on:

'If we could know when it would all end, we could plan
our lives for that date. We could plant in the fields knowing
what crops would be finished, what we could harvest in the
time before we went home. But there is a sense of futility
in all we do. We never know if tomorrow we will need what
we are doing today. If we plant today we do not know that
we will reap the harvest before we go home again, and perhaps many times.'

I stopped for a minute and sat up in my bunk and looked
across the prison camp. The moonlight played through the
tall tropical palms and across the corrugated iron roofs. I
went on with my imaginary letter:

'Perhaps you would like to know about the spotlight that
glistens along the barbed wire fence, and the thorns that
sparkle in the harsh light. These fences wind their way
around the camp attached to the living fenceposts of the
kapok tree, which we were obliged to plant when we first
came here.

'I know one of the questions you would like to ask is—do
we ever think of home? Do we think of you often? Yes, we
think of you. We think of home and the many things that
make up home for us.

'Besides our loved ones at home we think about the sound that a quarter makes when you flip it on a glass counter and ask for a package of cigarettes. Or the hustle and bustle and noise that comes to a city when the office hours are over and the men are rushing home. The feel of a starched white shirt when you run your hand down in the sleeve and it's slightly stuck together. The smell of good soap and hot water to bathe and shave with. It will be strange to us, having lived here in the jungle as we do, to hear again the honks of cars and the slap of their tires on the pavement.

'Yes, we are crowded here. There are many men. We laugh and talk, kidding each other about our life and the things we want to do when we get back home again. We have companionship here, but in it there is something lacking. Every man is lonely, for he misses those who love him most. He is lonely here, with all these men around him.

'The men here no longer wrap themselves in a cloak of pretence as we have to do in our everyday life when we are free. They are themselves, no better, no worse, than you would expect them to be, but they are themselves. And we have learned to accept each other.

'Men now discuss their past life with a freedom we would never expect if we were home. There are men here, good men, who in their past lives were politicians, doctors, mechanics. There are some who were gangsters. They talk about their life as the others do, with no apparent shame. Here they have become good men, for every man has learned to live close to death. And close to death most men are better.

'I have four very good friends here. I wish that you could visit their mothers and fathers. You would have so much

in common, and I know you would like them, for their sons
are good men. But, of course, I can't tell you these things.
I can only pretend to write this letter. I can't tell you of the
unusual tolerance here. Only yesterday a boy and I were
working in the field together and he told me an odd story
about his life. I'll only tell you his first name. It is Carl. As we
worked along, he said with a certain amount of sadness:

'"You know, Stew, I don't think I'll ever get to go home
alive. I've known for a long time," he went on, "that I'll never
go home alive."

'I looked over at him with surprise. As a rule we don't
allow the men around us to talk that way, because it lowers
our own confidence. It's a thing we will not face, the possi-
bility of not going back. But for some reason I did not feel
that I should stop him, because I knew he wanted to talk.

'"You know, Stew, I was just a boy of about twelve or
thirteen years of age," he said, "when a friend of mine and
I were driving out in the country hunting rabbits with our
.22's. We got into an argument over whether a .22 would
kill a man. And not too far away I saw a farmer walking
across his field. I'll never know what made me do it, but I
lifted the gun and I took careful aim and fired it.

'"When they found him the farmer was dead. My friend
and I, we never told what we had done. I never told anyone, and I knew my friend never did either. I went on with
my life, on through school, but you know, Stew, it's always
been with me. I know that I have to pay for that, and it
looks as though I'm going to have to pay for it pretty soon.
I don't know what will happen. I'll go on fighting to live,
but I feel sure that in the end I won't be allowed to go home
again."

'I won't say that his revelation did not shock me, but the thing that I know most was that now he could tell it with no fear because men here live without reprisal from their fellow-Americans. We live stripped of all pretence that we carry in normal life.

'I said nothing to Carl, for there was nothing to say. It was a ghost that he himself had to live with. But Carl was a close friend of Jamison, and I knew that Jamison thought a lot of Carl. And Jamison was a good man and had lived a very simple life. He had accepted Carl with his ghost in his background and loved him as only friends can who are prisoners many miles from home.

'You might like to know that the men have built up a certain immunity to some diseases, though many are often sick. The only medicine we ever receive is an occasional issue of quinine.

'I'd like you to know about a little Jewish doctor here in the prison who works all day in the fields with us. In his evenings, and on the free day that we have once a week, he spends his time helping the other men. He's a brilliant man. He has found that chewing the leaves of a certain tree will relieve a man from constipation, and certain little native herbs he has found will stop a man's diarrhoea. He's been a great help to us. He has saved many lives and we are all very proud of him.

'I could also tell you about the great work another man is doing, a Catholic priest. Regardless of the men's faiths, he talks to them, and most of all he lets them talk to him. They talk about their problems, their altered beliefs, their faith. And he gives each man more strength of purpose and a greater desire to do the right thing.

'Yes, I think that when this is all over, those of us that come home again will be better men. We'll be better, and we will feel that we have earned the right to do something with our lives. We cannot afford to waste, to throw away this wonderful gift, the luxury of living, if we are allowed to live and to come home again.

'You know how I've always loved to write. Well, I can't write here. Occasionally I make up a rhyme or a piece of poetry, but we have no paper. Once in a while one of the men who is working on some detail around the Japanese garbage dump will have the chance to tear the labels off empty cans. The back of the labels is white and clear. But this paper is very valuable, and most of it is used for keeping death records and burial lists of the men who die here. So we really have nothing on which we can keep a personal record of our experiences.

'There are things of beauty here. Things that you, mother, would appreciate most. I've never seen sunsets, not even in Oklahoma where the sun sets red and reflects across the hills, like those I see here, shining across the tops of the vast green jungle. Men have been allowed to bring various wild bulbs into the camp. Hanging above my head now is a cluster of orchids embedded in a piece of rotten wood. They are more beautiful than any orchids I have ever seen. And hanging from the rafters of every hut inside the prison camp are thousands of these orchids. In the cool shady side of the shacks, we have planted lily bulbs and many tropical flowers. They bloom all the time. I know you would like to have some in your garden at home.

'I know too that you worry a lot about my religion. I wish I could tell you how much more religious we have all be-

come. But it isn't a religion of fire and brimstone. It is a
religion of peace and quiet. It's true that the Japanese do
not allow us to have church services here in the prison. But
we are able to defeat them. The various chaplains hold little
meetings at night when it is dark. And there are prayer
meetings early every morning before the men go out to
work. So even though they suppress an open church service,
the Japanese have made us more defiant and stronger in
our belief. Even those who might not have attended the
services at all do so now, because they feel that they are
taking something from the Japanese. For whatever reason
they go to these little services we have in the middle of the
night, they take something away that is greater than themselves. So real good is accomplished.

'We have no books to read. Some of the men have Testa-
ments or Bibles which they have been able to hide from
the Japanese, but mainly our time is taken up in other ways.
Most of the men have little hobbies.

'My friend Hughes spends his time carving a pipe out of
camagon wood. Weldon has made a good many boats, very
beautiful with intricate detail. I've not done much with my
hands, but I spend a lot of time composing poetry in my
mind as I work in the fields. John is trying to learn to speak
another language. There is a Russian here in the camp and
he is teaching John to speak Russian.

'Rassmussen spends most of his time talking to men who
have been in various businesses. Already he's told me at least
fifty different types of business that he plans to go into after
the war is over. And tomorrow he will come to me with a
new idea. But all of it helps to occupy our time and keep
our minds fresh and clear. Because we often wonder if we

will be sane men when we come home again to live with men who have not been locked up, who do not know what it is to be locked away from the world for many years.

'There are funny things that happen. I wish that I could have had a picture of the beard I grew last year. It was curly and red. I was surprised that it was red, for my hair is dark. John grew a moustache for a while and then shaved it off. But Hughes and Weldon still wear theirs. Every day or so Weldon says he will cut his off.

'If you wonder what we use to shave with, I might say that the men have found various methods. Men pull long spikes out of the wood that holds the buildings together. They flatten them with stones and spend hours sharpening one side until it has a razor's edge. These are used to shave with. Only certain men possess these razors. You must trade something with them in order to use them.

'There are odd types of bartering going on, for our values are different than they would be otherwise. There is nothing we have here that does not have some value, for even a piece of string can be used. The cigarettes we get from the Japs are the currency we use. One man was able to trade a needle from a Jap and he unravels cloth for thread.

'The pants legs of our trousers went long ago. By sewing up one end, they make a handy bag in which to store our few belongings.

'A few weeks ago one of the Jap guards who has been friendly to me gave me a piece of soap. We use it only once a week, my friends and I. Usually on Sunday afternoons we take a bath with soap. I know it seems strange to have soap only once a week, but it does give a sense of luxury that we don't normally have.

'Yes, I know that at home you all hate the Japanese, and there is much to make you feel that way. But here we do not hate them perhaps as much as you do, because now most of us speak their language and we have learned to understand their superstitions, their beliefs, their religion, their way of life. Many of them are like men all over the world, no better, no worse. They too like to take out their photographs and show pictures of their wives and children. They too long for the war to end so they can go home again.

'Oh, yes, they are brutal. But it is the brutality of ignorance and superstition. I know that does not make the beatings hurt any the less, if one understands them. But understanding the Japanese, you cannot hate them any more than you can hate a man who is crazy, for he does not know why he does what he does. These Japanese have been taught their way of life for generations. They do not understand modern civilisation.'

Soon I fell asleep, but for many nights afterwards I lay there composing an imaginary letter to my mother and father, thinking of the things I would like to tell them.

At last they took us out of the prison camp at Davao and loaded us on boats. We headed north again to the island of Luzon. We landed in Manila during August of 1944. They rushed us through the city in trucks and north to Cabana-tuan. The place was much like the other camps had been, but there was less food now. However, rumours flew and our hopes were higher. We thought that surely we would be free soon. We had been prisoners so long.

We thought of home, talking of the things we wanted to do when we were free again, the things we wanted to see, the books we would read. Oh, how good it was to think of going home. Then, one day, the twenty-first of September, we were working in the rice fields when we heard a humming sound. It was like a swarm of bees. The sound grew stronger and stronger. We looked up into the sky and there were hundreds of planes, like tiny silver gnats high in the sky. We knew they were American planes. But no man could show his emotion, no prisoner dared show how thrilled he was. We kept our heads down and kept on working.

'Don't lose your heads now. Don't show anything because the Nips are trigger-happy. Act like you don't even see them,' Weldon commanded, and we kept quiet.

But I was so happy I felt I couldn't stand it. I was trembling all over. Those were our planes! The first American planes we had seen since 1941. I was weak all over as I listened to them. Freedom was close! We would be liberated surely within a few days, if there were so many planes.

The Jap guards began chattering around us, and finally ordered us out of the paddies. They kept their eyes on the sky as they herded us back inside the prison camp. We stayed inside the shacks for fear the guards would shoot in their nervousness. But we watched the planes through the cracks of the buildings.

We could hear the roar as bombs fell on the Jap airfields nearby. We put our arms around each other and danced with happiness, for we were to be free. Free at last! We patted each other on the backs, congratulating ourselves. It would be a matter of days, maybe hours.

Then our eyes flew to John, who had been strangely ill for some time. We felt sure what it was, for his cheeks were flushed and red and he ran a temperature, always in the afternoon. The slightest effort made him cough and his whole

body wracked and shook. Yet none of us would admit to the
others the disease he had. We knew we were racing with
time until the Americans arrived with medicine to save John.

In the night he coughed, and the groans of pain which
came through his clenched teeth hurt us all. One of us
would reach forward and hold his arm without speaking,
letting him know that we were there, and that we cared
because he was in pain. For his sake we were even more
thrilled that the American planes were in the sky.

That night we huddled together, whispering excitedly until the sun came up. But there were no more American
planes and we were led out to work again. We did not have
to see them now, for we had seen them once and that sight
was better than any rumour. The Americans were close. We
did not have to depend on rumours.

Each of us knew one guard who liked him better than he
did the other prisoners, whom he could talk out of cigarettes
and occasionally have a word with about how the war was
going. The minute I had the chance I sought out old Maurii.
When he had given me a cigarette I asked him about the
fighting.

'The Americans are very close. Soon we will move you all
to Manila,' he said in Japanese. 'And I hear they will take
all the American prisoners to Japan.'

My heart fell. Oh, no, surely they would not try to take
us out, not now! I could not tell my friends what Maurii
had said. I could not shake their belief and their hope of
freedom. But days went by, and weeks, and a month and
two months. Late in October they loaded us onto trucks.
There were many American planes in the air now.

We sped along the highway until we reached Manila.

They took us into the old Federal Prison there, herding us into the building and locking us by small groups in separate cells. Four of us were able to stay together, Rass, Weldon, Hughes and myself, but John had been shifted with one of the other groups and was locked in a different cell.

In our cell there was a huge window that opened into the outer compound. Steel bars ran across it to the ceiling and the ledge of the window was wide enough for a man to stand on. You could grab hold of the bars and pull yourself up and then you could look out across the walls and over the city and see the planes high in the air.

The Japanese no longer took us out to work as a group. Occasionally one man would be taken out for some clean-up detail, or to carry in the rice buckets or the water. Other than that, they kept us locked up, and we waited, watching the planes. And there were more and more planes in the sky every day.

2

One afternoon a guard came to our cell. He grunted and pointed at me. I had no idea what he wanted, but he unlocked the door and motioned for me to follow him.

I trailed behind him through the corridor and down the stairs. Then I saw Maurii standing at the door, waiting. My heart leaped up, for he had always treated me better than he had the other prisoners. All of the guards had prisoners they liked and would slip cigarettes to. I knew Maurii had asked for me and I was grateful. It would be good to go outside after being locked up in the cell for so long, no matter what the work was.

Maurii nodded impassively and turned. I followed him

through the door and into the compound. When we were
out of sight of the other guards he handed me a cigarette.
He pointed to a rake and indicated that I was to clean the
drains at the base of the prison walls. I started to work just
as one of the planes shot low over the prison and dived at
something beyond the walls. I turned and looked back at
Maurii.

He pulled his cap back off his close-cropped black hair
and squinted his eyes toward the sky. He leaned with his
hands closed on top of each other against his rifle. He sighed
then, and I wanted to ask him how he felt, knowing the
Americans were so close and coming closer every day. I
could not help feeling sorry for him. All that he had been
told and taught about the religious invincibility of the Japanese was being proved wrong. He turned his face toward
me sadly.

'It is true,' he said in faltering English, then lowered his
voice to a confidential whisper. 'The Americans have taken
Leyte—nearly six weeks already.'

I wanted to scream with joy, but I kept my face immobile.
Taking my eyes from the bewildered expression on his face,
I looked again at the American planes diving in the ice-blue
sky. So it was true. The American Army was only a hundred
and fifty miles away. Now I could understand why there
were so many planes in the sky. They were land-based planes
and more were coming every day.

I could have spent all my time staring at the sky. There
was a strange, exulting lift to my whole body. I wanted to
cry or laugh or yell all at once. The cruel cold years of waiting, hungrily waiting, fell from me like dead leaves in an
autumn wind. Each burst of anti-aircraft shelling was break-

ing the tight chains that had held me prisoner for so long. Soon I would be free. Free! Tears kept seeping into my eyes, and I looked back at the sky.

Like Chinese firecrackers, the anti-aircraft burst and floated off in tiny wisps of blue and white clouds until the sky was filled with a salt-and-pepper effect. I became anxious for the safety of the free and happy little planes that roared and buzzed apparently without a care. These planes were mine. They were part of me. No harm must come to them.

It was only when a plane zoomed alarmingly close, dropping almost beyond the prison walls, and the ground trembled with the explosion, that I realized their deadliness. I wanted to yell to them, 'You are free, free! Free as the air and the sky.' I wanted badly to see the faces of the crew, the glow and health and excitement they must hold.

When I finished my work the drains along the wall were running freely. Maurii led me back inside the building and delivered me to the guard at the door.

I told him my cell number, and he led me up the stairs and down the long corridor. The prisoners stared at me, eager to ask what news I had learned. I was the only prisoner who had been taken outside for any duty in the past two days, but they dared not speak until the guard had locked me in my cell again. The word would be passed along. The excitement would bounce from cell to cell. The prisoners would chatter like magpies and call to their friends in the other cell blocks. Now they were silent. Their silence intensified their hope and craving for news. Any news, even a hopeless rumour that they could pretend to believe, could take sides on and argue about during the endless hours.

Passing John Lemke's cell, I looked into his serious face

and smiled. His thin blue-white face and his dark encircled eyes carried the world's sadness, but he smiled as usual and the bright pink spots on his cheeks became brighter. The effort was too much, and he was taken with racking coughs which he desperately tried to control.

Oh, John, I wanted to whisper, you will be well again. Free and happy and well. How long now had our little group cared for John? Not even admitting to each other the evidence of his tuberculosis. It was strange, I thought. Rass, and Weldon and myself, even John had known all along that he was rotten inside with the disease. But as long as it was never brought into words, never mentioned, it was less real. How many times one of us had gripped John's arm when he was racked with coughs and was trying to breathe. We never put into words how much we cared, or how much we were betting on him to make it, and stay with us.

The guard unlocked the iron-barred door and held it open for me. The eyes of the men in the cell were fastened hopefully on my face. I heard the sound of the key in the lock and the hollow noise of the guard's steps receding down the hall before I spoke.

'Maurii says that Leyte has been in the Americans' hands for over six weeks now.' I tried to make the announcement as free from emotion as though I were discussing the weather, but my voice broke and I laughed.

There was a gasp from the group. Suddenly they all talked at once. Men ran to the bars and whispered the news to the other cells. The whispers rose to shouts, and the shouts to cheers. They were laughing and crying and dancing with each other in little circles in the crowded cells. Some were beating their friends on the back with wild enthusiasm.

'We've made it!' they yelled. 'It's only a matter of days, hours, until the Americans will have us free again.'

Suddenly the entire prison was quiet again. A cold wind of doubt had blown through the place, gripping each man. They must not believe this. There had been so many rumours, false hopes they had prayed for and believed in. They had passed and lay buried in the hungry years that were behind us. Now this new hope became suddenly a thing to be feared. No man could bear to be led down the old path of hoping and praying for a day that never came. Yet each man wanted to believe, and the rattling crack of the anti-aircraft was proof written in the sky for all to see.

My eyes flew to Rassmussen's face. He had been very quiet through the first outburst. We didn't speak, and his face was expressionless, but we understood each other. I glanced at Weldon and Hughes. They huddled in one corner of the room and they were whispering to each other with great animation. They had forgotten the rest of us. I walked over and stood by Rass and looked out of the window.

The window had a wide cement ledge that was about waist-high. The steel bars of the old prison rose straight and open to the high ceiling. I started to climb up, and Rassmussen gave me a boost and then climbed up beside me.

I let my hands close about the bars. The cold steel felt real and cruel. Below us lay the open compound that stretched to the high prison walls. A guard had left his little hut and was making his patrol along the top of the wide wall. In the sky there were more planes than we had ever seen before. Our planes, I thought. Back home in Oklahoma I had seen swarms of black crows circling above a corn field. These planes were very much like them.

'Stew,' Rassmussen's voice was low, almost a whisper.

'Yes, Rass.'

The sky was beginning to darken and the shell bursts began to make faint sparkles of fire against the darkness.

'God—God is good, isn't he, Stew?'

'Yes, Rass, God is awful good.'

We were silent a long time, each with our own thoughts.

Across the wall in the distance we could see the bay. Fires gleamed along the waterfront. In the mouth of the river and across the breakline could be seen black, ghost-like hulks of sunken or half-sunken ships, blasted by American bombs. Apparently the planes had left nothing afloat as far away as the eye could see. Beyond lay the ocean and the China Sea.

'They can never evacuate us now, to keep us from being liberated,' Rass said slowly.

I chuckled. 'Even a canoe couldn't float in that water, let alone to Japan—and now the Americans are only a few miles away.'

'Just a matter of days—maybe hours,' he muttered more to himself than to me. 'Maybe, even before Christmas.'

Oh, God, surely before Christmas. I began a rapid calculation. This must be the ninth of December, maybe the tenth, but I didn't want to turn and ask anyone in the room, for fear of revealing the intensity of my hope. There was no sunset, but just a faint glow of red that mingled with the fires of the city. The smoke floated rosy and purple and, as the sun slipped away, turned black. The fires burned on, licking their flames at the sky. The shells boomed away, filling the sky with huge Roman candles that burst and split in momentary blazes of beauty. The roar of our planes continued to be heard.

The next morning a small bundle of prisoner mail was brought into the building, the first we had ever seen. Since it came after the news of the day before, we began to feel that our captors were trying to be nice because they would soon be in our position. When the guard started down our side of the corridor with the diminishing bundle, I tried desperately not to be interested. If I didn't care, if I didn't want a letter so badly, maybe I would get one.

He called off in stammering Japanese the American names which were so hard for him to pronounce. Each time my heart leaped with hope. I could see the look on Rass' face. I knew how badly he wanted to hear from home. None of us had ever heard. The guards handed in only a few letters to each cell.

Hughes and Weldon stood together, trying not to show their interest, but it was written on their faces. When the guard reached our cell he handed in two letters. One was for Hughes. I swallowed my disappointment. I had wanted to know what had happened to my family. Had one of my brothers been killed in the war? Here it was nearly four years, and I had received no word from home.

Hughes grasped his little note, twenty-five words long, and walked off by himself. Weldon stayed in one of the corners, knowing that Hughes wanted to be all alone to read what little news he had received. Rass and I walked back to the window and took up our vigil—we were watching the destruction of the city. When I looked back, I saw Hughes' face.

He had a look of incredulity, and tears were forming in his eyes. He came over and without saying a word handed me the note that he had received. It was from his mother.

'I'm learning to drive a car now, your father is dead, and I am managing the ranch.'

I didn't know what to say. He crawled up in the window beside us. Finally he began to talk without looking at either of us.

'You know, she has never worked. She has always been taken care of and protected. She never learned to drive a car and now she's learning. There's no one there to help her. No one to show her what to do.'

I saw his hands whiten as he gripped the bars, as if he would have liked to tear them apart. If only he could get back! She needed him. He was an only child.

'It won't be long now,' he went on. 'Then I'll be there and I can help her. She'll never have to worry.' Then quietly, 'Oh, why did we ever have to leave England?'

I wanted to help him, but words seemed futile. Hughes jumped down from the window-ledge, walked over to the corner and handed the note to Weldon. I felt that to have no word was better than to have known what Hughes had learned. At least I didn't know, but I could hope that nothing had gone wrong in my long absence.

Each day was much the same. There was no more mail. Every day the guards dragged an old iron tub, clanging and bumping, along the cement floor. At each cell they ladled out a mere handful of rice. There was not enough food value in the little cup of watery rice we received each day to keep us more than just sleepily alive.

I was dizzy and tired. If I got to my feet suddenly I blacked out and grasped at something to keep from falling. My legs were beginning to swell with beri-beri. There was a glazed look in many of the men's eyes. There was an

almost stupid attempt to focus attention at times on the
conversation around them.

There were mutterings and childish bickerings. None of
us was normal. Some felt that when we were free, we would
all be classed as insane. We had been so many years without
seeing normal men. How would we appear to men who had
not been in prison for all these years? There was a fear
that everyone of us had turned odd and strange. Our sense
of values had changed. Life had gone on without us.

I awoke one night to feel a cool moist wind blowing inside
the cell block, and rain pattering along the ledge. Occasionally a drift of it would spatter across the floor. It was getting
cold and chilly. I tried to sleep again, but the cold moaning
sound of the wind across the city kept coming towards me.
I wondered if the rain would put out the fires left by the
planes the day before. Now there were no sounds of planes
and no sound of anti-aircraft bursting in the sky. There was
only the soft moaning of the wind and the patter of the rain.

When morning came and the early light felt its way
through the iron bars I could see that there was no sun. It
was still gloomy and overcast and the wind was still blowing. While waiting for our food I walked to the window and
looked out. The skies were heavy and thick and fog floated
and obliterated the bay. I could see just as far as the outer
walls of the compound. The rain was coming down in sheets.
Gradually the wind grew stronger and stronger until it
reached a moaning pitch, a lament for the city that was being
destroyed.

All through the day it rained as the wind mounted. Sometimes it blew a fine spray through into our rooms until many
of us were soaked. Through the night it rained. The next

day it was still raining, but in the afternoon the rain began to abate. It ceased raining and the wind stopped. Still the sky was overcast, and the clouds hung low over the city.

No planes could fly overhead, and I could see only a short distance because the fog along the bay was floating up the Pasig River. But I could see the city and the gutted buildings. Their black hulks were like gaunt skeletons. There was no more rain that day and no more wind, but the clouds did not part and you heard no planes at all.

Through the night I kept thinking and watching. I began to fear now what might happen. There was something ominous in the air, as though the storm was cheating us. The next morning the clouds were still overhead, and there were no planes.

At noon Jap officers and enlisted men ran up and down the corridors screaming, 'Kushma! Kushma!' They said we were leaving, and to prepare to move quickly. We could not believe it. No man would face the effort. He could not stand to put into words the fear or the blasted hopes.

The Japanese unlocked each cell and led us in columns of four through the corridors and down the stairs and out into the open compound. I stood with my group of friends. None of us was speaking. We listened to the jabbering of the interpreters and the coarse screams of the guards. I searched the sky. Every man begged the clouds to part, the sun to shine, the planes to return. Then they would not be able to get us out. I could see Father Cummings standing not too far away and I looked at him. Maybe if he would pray, something would happen to prevent all of this.

Maybe they were merely moving us somewhere else in the city, where it was less dangerous. This idea floated about and was repeated among the men. Surely no ship could have come in. The storm had lasted three days. No ship could have reached Manila. Even though there were no planes in the air, it was too short a time.

'Yes, that is right,' every man said. They were merely moving us to a safer place. Maybe to the suburbs, out of the city, where there would be less chance of our being hit by our own planes.

Yashamura, the Jap doctor who had always tried to be kind, stood before us. He spoke in clipped but distinct English as he told us that they had brought a ship in and that we would be taken to Japan. We would be safe. We had nothing to fear. They were taking out as well the Japanese civilians and their families. There would be women and children and the boat would be marked. We had nothing to fear.

Nothing to fear! I wanted to laugh hysterically. There was nothing that we feared as far as the boat was concerned. It wasn't that. It was the fact that we were so near being free. And now freedom was being blasted from us. Again we would have to swallow the heartbreak of wasted hopes.

Within an hour we were ready to go, each man with his pitifully small bundle of personal belongings. None of us with shoes on our feet. We walked with what little we owned held in our hands. We carried old ketchup bottles, cans or whatever containers we could get to hold water. We started out. They opened the gates of the old prison. Then we were in the middle of the street.

There was very little traffic now. Even the little caramata ponies were gone. The rickshaw had returned to Manila. We walked through the streets slowly, each man dragging his feet, heavy and dropsied with beri-beri, and weak from the days of starvation. Yet there was excitement in the city, for many of the buildings still burned and cast sparks down upon the street. There was debris everywhere, and little had been done to clear it away.

We passed down Rizal Boulevard and reached the foot of the Quezon Bridge. I was surprised to see that it had not been destroyed. I was near the front of the column and could look back at the straggling group of broken-hearted men stretching behind us. There were slightly over sixteen hundred of us in this group.

As I reached the other side of the bridge, I looked to my left. There was nothing but a heap of rubbish where once had stood the beautiful old castle of Estado Mayor, the castle where I had lived before the war started. It stretched away, gutted and bare, to the edge of the river. This castle was now only piles of mortar and dust. A few remaining walls stood alone, propless, as though at the push of a child's hand they would tumble to the ground.

We passed on through the streets and there was a look of sadness and pity on the faces of the Filipinos. We tried to make them feel we were brave, and that they must be brave. Americans would come again, they were near. Occasionally a Filipino threw a piece of food or a handful of candy into the crowd, but the guards chased him down and beat him.

We passed near the old walled city of Manila, a quarter that had stood long before the coming of the white man. It had thick walls and a filled-in moat and it was surrounded by huge flame trees aburst with red blossoms. It was a strange sight of beauty amid destruction and gloom and fear and hunger.

We marched across the open compound of the destroyed

church of Santo Domingo, and reached the pier. They lined us up among the ruins of what had been one of the world's most beautiful and largest piers, the Manila Pier Seven. Its white marble columns were ruined by the constant bombing. Across the ceiling stretched the skeleton steel structure and above it the open sky. I saw the boat then. It was a large boat, a converted Japanese luxury liner. But there would be little luxury for us on that ship.

The Japanese women and children passed us, laughing, carrying their boxes, dressed in their native costumes, flashing their fans. They walked by us as though we did not live, as though we were nothing more than the rubble scattered about the place. The guards allowed us to sit down and we waited for the final loading of the ship.

Soon the guards came down and walked among us, dividing us into three groups about equal in number. They began herding us like cattle up three different gangplanks and across the bow of the ship. Rass stood beside me as the others began to climb down through the hatch and into the hold.

'We thought that they'd never get us out.' There was a sob in his voice. He was holding John, who was now almost too weak to stand.

John smiled bravely. 'It'll be all right,' he said with effort. 'We'll be all right when we get to Japan.'

'We'll get more food. We'll be treated better,' I said hopefully.

Together we lifted John and began working our way down into the hold. When it was nearly full, guards came down and with whips began beating us farther back into the hold until it looked as if no more men could get in. Surely they could put no more men down. Yet more and more were coming. The ceilings were low, only about five feet high, but we were made to stand. We were packed, hunched down, until within two hours they had put more than six hundred men in an area not large enough to hold a hundred.

We were crammed so tightly that if a man fainted he could not fall to the floor. He would be packed between the men around him. One of the guards had told us that it would take only about ten days to get to Japan. Well, we couldn't live like this for ten days.

Surely after they put out to sea they would let us on the decks of the ship, let us have air. Gradually the air was becoming foul. It was getting hard to breathe, and there was only a small air hole, a small hatch opening. I started to sweat and I could feel the water draining out of me. I was dying for a drink of water. The air was becoming harder and harder to breathe.

Rass shifted John's weight to me and I held him up. He fainted and then he came to and fainted again. He was very weak and dying for air. He could no longer cough. He tried but it was a pitiful, almost whining sound that came from his lungs.

I prayed for the boat to start. Oh, how I wished Father Cummings was standing next to me. If he was where I could touch him I wouldn't be half as afraid. If only they headed out across the bay towards the China Sea. Surely then we would have air.

It was getting hotter and hotter. The hold was now an inferno. Men began to cry, begging for water. Cries for water went up all over the hold. A Jap guard appeared at the hatch above our head and shouted down into the hold.

'If you are not quiet, we will close the hatch cover. We will tighten down the hatches and you will have no air.'

Panic struck each man. We were suffocating, but what would happen if they shut off all the air? Only a matter of minutes and we would be dead.

It was late in the afternoon, nearly five o'clock.

I thought I could hear the noises of the ship starting up and the huge engines drumming. Then I saw the movement of light shadows cast down in the hold. I knew that we had started across the bay. The prisoners were screaming, crying for air and begging for water. Their cries were like those of tortured animals.

And today was the day we had thought to be free.

9 En Route to Japan: December 1944

AS THE SHIP started across the bay, I thought the movement would draft air down in the hold to us. I sweated constantly. I could hardly breathe. My head felt dizzy, my eyes were dim. I felt as though I was swimming up through a mossy pool, fighting for air, my lungs bursting. Suddenly I heard Weldon's voice and I turned. He was slapping Hughes' face.

'You fool!' he commanded. 'You fool! You must hold on. Try to be calm.' He slapped Hughes' face again and again. I thought he was too harsh, but gradually I saw the clearness return to Hughes' eyes.

Hughes shook his head and said, 'I'm sorry, I'm sorry.'

It seemed strange to me that a man should feel sorry for a thing he could not help. Sorry that he was human. Then I began to lose consciousness again. The weight of the suffocation and the foul odour began to press down on me. I was getting dizzy and seemed to be swimming again.

All of a sudden I felt myself being shaken. In the distance I could hear someone calling to me, calling, calling. As though down a long tunnel I heard my name, 'Stew! Stew! Stew!'

I tried to fight upward again for air. I was dying for a

taste of cool air. Suddenly I was clear again. Rass had turned his face toward me. He was calling me.

'Sid, try to hold on. Don't let yourself go. Try not to think of breathing. Just hold every ounce of yourself calm. If we keep complete control of ourselves we will be able to make it.'

The determination in his voice gave me strength again. I shook my head to clear it and then ran my hand across my face and down the skin of my chest. The skin felt rough and flabby as if I had been immersed in hot dishwater for several hours. It was wrinkled and wet with my own sweat.

'Help me to hold John up. I think he's going,' Rass said. 'I'm afraid he can't last much longer.' The words seemed to be torn from him as if it was more than he could bear.

Our friend. We had tried so long to protect him and keep him alive. We had prayed so hard that he should live. He seemed to be going. I tried to wedge him in between us and we held him, placing his arms around our necks. Rass tried talking to him, tried screaming in his ear, hoping that he could hear. Finally John came back for just a moment. The pain in his eyes was terrible.

I tried to concentrate on his pain. I had been told by Father Cummings that if I could only fasten my greatest worry on to someone else, I would forget myself.

By now the screams for water were maddened screams. Sometimes I heard hysterical laughing, like that of a crazy woman, high-pitched and broken with sobs. Then there would be mumbled prayers all around. I knew Father Cummings was somewhere on the boat but I couldn't see him.

I did not know how long we had been down in the hold. But I could see that it was darker, so that it was surely night. The men began screaming and fighting. They tore at each other, they fought and pushed. Their screams of terror and their laughter were terrible things.

Suddenly there was more room. The fainting and the dead were sliding down until men littered the floor underneath our feet. We had more room to move in. But under our feet were the bodies of men.

I could feel the flesh of a man's body beneath me. I was standing on him and it was awkward to move. I knew I must hold on. I put my arm around John and I felt that he was warm and still alive. He came to again. In the faint light he looked sadly at the other men. That they should destroy themselves at a time like this. That they should attempt to kill each other.

The men fought on. The dizziness came back to me again, the feeling of being sucked under, sucked down. I felt myself losing consciousness. Then, through a great distance, I heard the sound of someone weeping. They were sobs of someone very dear to me. I cannot stand it, I thought. The sobs were like those of my brother, or my father. I fought myself hard, and regained consciousness.

I could see in the faint gloom that Rass was weeping. Sobs shook him all over. Then I knew, because he held John so tenderly, that John had died.

John was dead. His long fight was over. He would never have to fight again. Never again would he be beaten or hungry. He was free, his soul was free. But Rass wept.

We debated a moment what to do with the body.

'I can't bear to think of his being trampled beneath our feet here. But we can't hold him much longer,' Rass said.

Finally we laid him beneath us and Rass stood on him.

At moments my mind was lucid and clear, horribly clear,

and I grasped the horror of our situation. I lost consciousness several times. During the night Weldon reached over and shook me.

'You must be careful.' His voice was grave. 'Do not let anyone touch you that you don't know and don't let anyone get too close to you. Men are killing each other in the hold around us. Listen!'

I heard strange noises. Men were choking each other. Then the awful truth dawned on me as I looked at a body lying beneath me on the floor. His throat had been cut and the blood was being drunk.

A new terror flowed into my heart now, a fear for my life. I began to distrust even those standing close to me. I looked at Rass with a strange horror. Could he? Could he do a thing like that to me? Then I looked at Weldon and at Hughes. On their faces was written the same distrust of each other. God, what were we becoming?

A few feet away I saw two men grappling. In the gloom I recognized who they were. They were father and son. I remembered how they had protected and cared for each other in the years past. They were both West Point graduates. The son was killing his father. I could see the look in the father's eyes. A look of compassion and pity for the son who was a maniac.

Terror ate into my soul. If I lost consciousness again anything could happen. I might be destroyed by the friends around me, by the people I loved. Yet, when I looked at the eyes of Weldon and Hughes and Rass, I knew that they were keeping their sanity.

When the first faint light of morning penetrated through the circling gloom into the hold, I began to pray that we would receive water and air. I noticed that there was a faint difference in the light that was coming into the hold. Mingled with it was a sparkle. I knew the sun was in it, and that above us the sun was shining.

The sun was shining! Planes could again circle in the air above us. The men were still fighting with each other and screaming like maniacs. I heard the gentle weeping of Hughes and I turned. Weldon was talking to him.

'But why can't I drink it?' Hughes said. 'Why can't I drink it?' he asked, in the petulant voice of a little boy. He had urinated in a bottle. 'It's got water in it,' he said. 'It won't hurt me.'

Weldon was cautioning him against it, but on his face was a question. Could it be done? Could a man drink his own urine?

I looked over at Rass and on his face was the same thought. From somewhere in the past I remembered a story of two prospectors caught in the middle of the desert. In their desire for water one man had drunk his own urine and died. Was that story true? I didn't know. How could the author have known? Had he ever seen such a thing? We needed water, our throats burned with the desire for a little moisture.

Hughes lifted the bottle and drank in one large choking gulp. He turned white and quickly began to retch. The thought came to me, 'He must not die!' He retched and retched. At last he was better.

Suddenly from the depths of the hold I heard a voice like the voice of God. Father Cummings began to speak. The sound was clear and resonant and made me feel he was talking to me alone. The men became quiet.

'Our Father Who art in heaven, hallowed be Thy name.

Thy kingdom come. Thy will be done on earth as it is in heaven. . . .' The voice went on. Strength came to me as I listened to the prayer, and a certain calmness of spirit.

'Have faith,' he continued. 'Believe in yourselves and in the goodness of one another. Know that in yourselves and in those that stand near you, you see the image of God. For mankind is in the image of God.'

For a while sanity returned to the faces around me. Then slowly the wails and cries began to rise again. But some of us continued to be held by the strength in that voice, the voice of a man who believed and who wanted us to believe. Through him we had faith in God and faith in our fellow man.

I heard someone yell and I looked toward the centre of the hold. Commander Bridgets was looking up the ladder at the Jap guard who stood above. I could not see the guard, but I knew that orders had been given that anyone who laid a hand upon the ladder leading from the hold would be shot immediately.

'I'm coming up!' Bridgets said sternly, in a voice used to command.

I saw him lay his hands on the ladder. Slowly he put one foot on the first rung and then on another one. A shot rang out. He fell back, gripping the steel ladder with all his might.

'I said I was coming up and I am coming up!' he said with determination. He started again and I tensed myself, waiting for the next shot. It didn't come. Then I heard him reach the top of the ladder. He was pleading with the guards to allow us to have water and to throw back the hatch covers so we could have air. He begged them in the name of humanity for these things. His voice became dim and I could hear little of it.

Somehow the rumour had been tossed into the hold that one of the ships in the convoy had been attacked during the night by submarines and that we were heading again toward the shore. God! Then perhaps we could get out of this hold.

Suddenly I heard Commander Bridgets speaking again. He seemed completely cool and it was like an announcer calling the plays of a sport.

'I can see two planes,' he yelled back into the hold. 'I can see two planes going for a freighter off on our starboard side,' he said. 'Now two more are detached from a formation in the sky. I think they may be coming for us. They are! They're diving. Duck everybody! Duck everybody!' he screamed.

Then I heard the roar of the planes overhead. 'Duck,' I thought. 'Duck where?'

Suddenly the guns opened up from our ship. The anti-aircraft clacked away, shaking the boat with the rattle.

'They're bombing!' someone screamed.

A bomb struck topside and the boat danced and shook. I could hear the roar of the planes overhead and the clattering of their machine guns as they circled and dived above us. There was the steady roar of their motors and a screaming, zooming noise as they dived again and again. The ship trembled convulsively with each impact of the bombs. I wondered what would happen if one of the bombs should strike dead centre into the hold. None of us could survive. Then I heard Commander Bridgets speak again in his clear commanding voice.

'You have nothing to fear. You have only your lives to lose.'

'Only my life,' I thought. Yes, that's right. Only my life.

'You have nothing to fear,' he went on. 'After all, if they hit dead centre here, it's the end and you've sat so close to the end for so long that it should not matter now. Try to think. Try to feel that it doesn't matter,' he said.

I tried to make myself feel that it didn't matter, that in another moment I might be in eternity. Down inside me I knew it did matter. But strangely, the thing I desired most was air and water. If I should die, I should no longer want those things.

The men's crying had turned to screams of terror. The heat of the fight overhead began to reach us. Guns clattered on the decks, and the lack of air became more oppressive. I had a dizzy feeling again. I was being pulled by an undertow far below the surface. I fought back, my head swimming. Whatever happened, I must hold on to consciousness. I must know what was going on about me, even the horror of it, so that I could protect myself.

I thought of a game I used to play when I was a little boy. Someone had told me that there was a little man who sat in a chamber above my eyes. He threw little switches that made every part of my body work. Lying in bed, stretched out calmly, I would play that the little man was moving my eyes by throwing a switch. Then I would play that I was going to keep him from moving my finger or my big toe. I couldn't keep him from doing it because as he threw the switch I would playfully lift my toe or raise a finger. I knew that the little man was the stronger.

I began to play that game now with intensity, for my very life. The little man sat there in the chamber, looking out through the holes that were my eyes, watching what was going on. Yet he wasn't a part of it. It was a terrible scene he was watching. I pretended that he moved my head so that he could look around. He could move my body any way he wanted and he could make me feel what I wanted. I would not die. I would feel no terror. The little man could not control other people, but he was controlling me. He would throw the right switches at the right time.

I heard Commander Bridget's voice again and he said, 'The ship is not too far from land. I believe we are at Subic Bay. Yes, it's Subic Bay!' he called down.

Then I heard a rifle shot and a crashing sound as his body tumbled back into the hold upon the men below.

A Japanese officer appeared at the hatch opening and yelled down to us.

'As soon as the guards are notified,' he said in English, 'we will allow you to come up and swim ashore. The boat is sinking.'

I felt the settling urge within the ship and I smelled thick pungent smoke. The ship was on fire. Oh, God, they must get us off soon. Again I heard planes diving upon us.

2

With an exploding scream the bombs crashed against the ship. More smoke was seeping down into the hold. I wondered what was happening to my friends in the other holds of the ship. Were they burning alive? I wondered. Were they all dead now? Many were dead around me in the hold, and more were dying all the time.

The clattering of the anti-aircraft on board the ship began again. The whole ship shuddered and jerked convulsively as the bombs struck, shattering against the decks. I heard no more Jap voices yelling into the hold, but word came through that the ship was burning badly and the captain of the ship might try to run it aground. We were not too far off shore. Then I heard the clattering of fifty-calibre machine guns ringing a rat-tat-too across the sides of the ship. Aeroplane machine guns were armour-piercing and could pierce the sides of a ship. It was getting dark down in the hold, the glow of evening remained for a moment, then that too was gone.

It was pitch dark, a slimy filth of darkness was about us and the squashy feeling of the bodies under our feet. Men were weeping again. Explosions shook the topside and sparks flashed into the hold. We were trapped alive. The thick burning odour was becoming heavier and heavier. We would be burned or drowned. Suddenly the ship gave another convulsive lurch and we were standing lopsided.

'It looks like it's about to go down now,' Weldon said calmly. There was no feeling in his voice. I realized the Japs were afraid we might try to make a rush for it and fight our way out. They were stationing more guards around the top and were closing down the hatches.

The filth and body stench was choking us. My friends no longer talked. We trusted each other and we hoped—that was all. Soon we heard that men were smothering to death back in the extremities of the hold.

Those of us who had shirts began to fan the air back to the rear so that the men behind us could breathe. They were suffocating and that took our minds off ourselves. Every man who could took off his shirt or trousers and fanned, hoping it would cause a suction in the air above.

All night this went on in the darkness. Men died and crazed men moved about, crying as though they were searching for something lost. I worried again for my life. Suddenly I heard Rass at my side.

'We've got to try to make it some way. We've got to take a chance,' he said to the three of us. 'We'll never live if we stay here. It's evident they're not going to let us get off. Men are organizing themselves, those that are sane enough to try it. We're going to fight our way up the hold.' Rass lowered his voice to a whisper. 'There's a pole near me, about five feet from us,' he said. 'I can't see it, but I know it's there, and it leads straight up out of the hatch. Can you all climb?'

'Sure,' Weldon grunted.

But I didn't know. I felt so terribly weak. I didn't know if I could climb. And I knew they'd shoot us if we tried it. By now it was morning and I could see the faint light again coming down through the opening.

'Let's go,' Weldon whispered.

We began working, holding ourselves together. We had to step between two crazed men. Using our fists, we slashed at their panic-stricken faces, forcing them apart. At last we reached the high rod that led up out of the hold. All around I could see men moving, trying the same thing in all the four corners, converging, some toward the ladders, some toward the other poles that led up out of the hold.

Rass reached the rod first and grasped it with his hands.

'The damned thing's damp,' he said. 'Water has condensed along it from the steam of the hold.'

I wished I was in his place. I wanted to lick the coolness

of that iron rod. Then I realized it was a foolish thought. First of all we must get out. We had to get out!

Above me I heard the planes, circling and diving again. A horrible crashing of bombs on the ship caused a lurch and I fell. As my knees went out from under me I felt Weldon's arms grab me. He lifted me to my feet again.

'I'm going up,' Rass said.

I saw him move, gradually pulling himself up. He gripped the rod with his knees and inched up slowly. I grasped the rod and began to work myself up just behind him, his feet touching my head. Slowly we moved on up. Then came Hughes. Behind him Weldon was giving instructions and cautioning him. We moved upwards out of the hold, trying to be quiet. We prayed that the men below would make enough noise so that the guards would not notice that we were edging toward the top.

Rass reached the edge first and grabbed it with his fingers. Then slowly he lifted one foot over, and dropped down on the outside. Before I reached the top he pulled back part of the hatch cover. The guards were trying to avoid the strafing of the planes overhead and they did not see him.

The light was coming in on the men below me as I reached the top. With every ounce of effort I pulled myself over. I thought I couldn't make it, but somehow, there I was. I stood up and reached for Hughes and gave him a quick jerk, helping him up. As his feet landed on the deck we ducked down again because of the guards. They were still lying flat to avoid being hit.

Then I heard the planes coming toward us again and I threw myself down. They missed us, strafing the superstructure. Weldon's head appeared and soon he was on deck beside us. We threw the hatch covers back and loosened the canvas. I watched a faint hope appear on the faces below. Sanity returned to their eyes as the air and light rushed down upon them.

Rass edged himself toward a piece of jagged steel that had been blown on the deck.

'Try to find a weapon,' he whispered hoarsely.

The guards jumped to their feet and looked down in the hold. On the other side men were coming up. The Japs lowered their guns on them and started shooting. Quickly Rass ran up behind them. I heard a crunching sound as a Jap's neck was broken. With a piece of steel Rass began chopping away at another guard and I grabbed one, wrestling with him. I knocked him off balance and pushed him screaming down the hold. They tore him apart down there. Hughes and Weldon took the last one.

By this time more men had reached the deck and more were swarming up the ladders. White-faced men came out of the other holds like freed animals. The sharp pungent odour of burning phosphorus from the bombs raked at my raw throat while black smoke belched from the portholes and the rear of the ship was enveloped in flames. Above, the sky was an ice-blue. There was an odd silence, now that the anti-aircraft was dead. I could see that the Nips had seen us, but they didn't seem to pay any attention. Their anxious eyes were searching the sky.

The happy thought came to me, 'They think we have been given permission to come up.' In the distance I could see the faint green haze of the shore line. I knew I couldn't make it. But I had to make it.

'I hope you buzzards can swim,' Rass said.

'Well, I'm not gonna do any fancy strokes for you,' I said.

'I wonder if there's water on this thing,' Weldon looked around. 'It isn't going down so fast. There might be water.'

The prisoners were sweeping over the ship, fighting with the Japs. Shooting started from above as they realized that open mutiny had broken out. Then I heard an ominous roar as the planes turned back and started diving.

'My God, we've got to get off this damned thing!' Hughes yelled as we rushed for the railing.

When I looked down into the water it was filled with Americans, their white bodies gleaming against the green.

Hughes was already undressed and Weldon reached for the railing and swung himself over. It looked far down to the water, but in a moment I had my clothes off and without stopping to look I pushed myself into a dive.

I felt the water close over me. Nothing had ever felt so cool, so refreshing as that water, so wonderfully soothing to my strained muscles. I opened my eyes and through the greenness the light shone on the water above me. I started fighting upward and my head burst through the water. The air seeped hard and clean down into my lungs, filling them with freshness and coolness.

'I can't swim! Help! Help!'

I couldn't go to anyone's help. Normally I could have saved a drowning man, but not now. I had only strength enough for myself and I closed my ears. Then I heard the planes in the air above us again and the rattling trat-trat-trat of machine guns. Someone in the water beside me screamed again.

'They're strafing the water! They're strafing us!'

Quickly I dived beneath the water again, going down, down. When my eyes opened I saw only a faint glimpse of the green light above me. Then my head burst above the water. The planes had passed but around me the water was red with blood. Bodies half-floated, riddled by the strafing of the planes.

Rolling over, I looked back at the ship. Prisoners were throwing pieces of hatch covers and anything that would float to the men who could not swim. I heard the planes again and looked around. One flew straight toward me and I noticed that it was dropping something. Little silver flags were falling toward the water. I saw the first one hit and it exploded. Then I knew what they were. They were small bombs.

'My, God!' I screamed. We were trapped like cornered animals. If I dived beneath the water, the concussion would crush me. I tried to place my body on the level of the water as the bombs began to explode around me. Then I heard the strafing again and I dived again, this time trying to get farther below the surface. When I fought myself up again I knew I was too weak. I could never make it. This constant diving beneath the surface was taking all my strength. I determined to strike out anyway and pray that they wouldn't hit me.

'I don't think I can make it,' Hughes called weakly. 'Please don't go on without me.'

Rass and Weldon were talking to him but afraid to get near him. In his frantic desire for life he might grab them and pull them both under.

There was a body near me and I reached for it. No! It wasn't a body. It was wood! It was a jagged piece of hatch cover. I pushed it over near Hughes. He grabbed it and a look of relief came into his eyes. It would not support more than one man. We struck out for the shore, swimming.

The water was bloody with the bodies of men killed by the strafing. I heard the rat-tat-tat of machine guns and I rolled over on my back and looked back at the ship. They were firing at us from the top of the ship with machine guns.

There was a desperate groan near me. It was Doctor Sullivan, the old Colonel. I headed toward him, fearing to get too close. He was trying hard but he was weak. I swam near him.

'If you'll let me help you. If you won't fight,' I pleaded with him. 'Just let me put my hand around your neck. I can grasp you that way and if you'll swim on your back and kick your feet I'll help you get to shore, but if you grab me I'll have to hit you. I can't let you grab me.'

'Please trust me,' he groaned, and his eyes begged.

I reached for him and as my hand closed about his neck I could feel him relax. Then we started swimming, the Colonel kicking his feet.

Pretty soon Rass yelled, 'Are you all right, Stew?'

'Okay,' I yelled back, surprised by my second wind.

It was a terrific distance, but the air was fresh and the water felt cool to our bodies after so many hours in the hold. At least drowning would be a clean death.

The shore was getting closer and I knew we could make it. All of a sudden the planes came back and they were in formation as they swept low over the water. I strained to see their faces, hoping that they could tell who we were. But the strafing went on and they were dropping their bombs. I knew I could not dive below again. If I was hit, that would be the end. I kept going, kicking my feet, and Colonel Sullivan worked beside me, struggling.

The prisoners were crowding in the water ahead of us. They stopped swimming and I could not understand why they were not going on to the shore. I looked ahead and saw that there was not a proper beach at all, but a high sea wall about eight feet high. On the wall there were Jap soldiers and their rifles cracked while bullets sang into the water, making the prisoners stay back. They were afraid that if the men got too close they would climb the wall and escape into the undergrowth.

Gradually they allowed us to move in. We began swimming, inching closer to the wall. The Jap guards lowered their guns, carefully playing them across us, in a warning not to try anything. With joyous relief my feet touched the sand beneath me and I stood up, lifting Colonel Sullivan. My eyes searched the crowd of naked white men for my friends. When I saw them they rushed forward. Rass grabbed me around the neck, and I knew how glad he was that I'd made it. Weldon gripped my hand and pounded me on the back. Hughes had tears in his eyes.

'I was afraid something bloody awful had happened to you,' he said.

I looked around for some of my other friends. One had died in the hold and another had drowned, they told me. Others had been cut to pieces by the strafing of the planes.

Jamison, a man out of my organization, laid his hand on my shoulder. When I looked into his eyes I sensed a horrible loss and sadness. I knew without asking that something had happened to his closest friend, Carl. I told him about John's death, hoping when I had finished he would tell me about

Carl, who had always said he would never make it home because of his boyhood crime.

'You know when we had to leave, the back hold was burning and steel girders fell down on the men,' Jamison said huskily. I had the feeling he was trying not to cry. 'One of the beams fell on Carl and he was pinned beneath it. He was going to be burned alive. I tried to pull him out. I tried awfully hard, but I couldn't get him out from under it.' Then Jamison's body began to shake with sobs and he kept running his fingers through his wet hair. 'I didn't know what to do. He wanted me to kill him. I didn't want to leave him, but I had to get away. I just left him. He cried for me to kill him. He didn't want to be burned alive. But I had to leave the ship and I couldn't kill him.' He looked up, his eyes searching my face for an answer.

'That's all right, Jamison,' I said. 'That's all behind us now. The ship out there is burning all our past, all that went on in that hold. We've got to forget it. We've got to trust each other now and forget what the men became in that hold.' I looked into his eyes, trying to convince him. 'Carl is gone and you couldn't do anything.'

I reached over and patted him on the shoulder and he went on sobbing. I knew pretty soon he would try to forget, and we would go on.

I was still terribly thirsty. I could see some of the men trying to drink the ocean water. Those who were more rational were cautioning the others about drinking the water. They began to beg the Nips on the sea wall above us to get water for us. But they stood there, immobile and silent, glaring down upon us and holding their guns levelled.

Then I heard the planes coming back. Nothing could

save us now. Some of the prisoners yelled and moved their hands above their heads, waving and jumping. Then the leading plane broke off from the formation.

I gritted my teeth and dug my fingernails into the palms of my hands, expecting any minute to hear the cutting of the plane's guns. But he didn't shoot. He levelled off and waved his wings back and forth. Then he signalled to the planes behind him and they did the same thing. They circled low again and the men kept yelling and waving their hands. This time the planes circled very low, almost skimming the water.

They know who we are at last, I thought. They know we are Americans. They cut away into their formation and straightened out and shot back toward the jungle and across the mountains going home. Going home!

I wondered how they must feel, knowing that they had killed many of us. But they couldn't have known at the time. It couldn't have been helped. But how they must feel now, I thought.

Exhausted, we slumped down at the base of the sea wall and waited, hoping that the Nips would give us water and medical attention. Many of the men were wounded and a man near me had his arm torn off.

Hours passed, and the sun was hot. Occasionally a white bumping form would float toward the shore. I searched for Father Cummings. I had not seen him and I wondered if he had got off the ship.

Time and again, a crazed American would attempt to climb the green, moss-covered wall, but each time he would be shot. It was hopeless. We tried to take care of the insane, talk sense to them, try to bring them back to reality. To reality when there was none.

In the middle of the afternoon one of the little guards yelled down to us and said that we would be allowed to come up. We started moving up and I lifted a wounded man near me and helped him. We struggled through the water and to the edge of the wall and began climbing.

We lined up on top of the sea wall and the Japs made us count off. There were more than twelve hundred men still alive. Many more than I expected. Finally word was passed along that we were going to be led into a little city called Olongapoo. It was only about a mile's walk from where we were.

We started out, straggling along, the brush and over-growth scratching our bare skin, with the Nips lining the area around us.

10 Tennis Court, Olongapoo, Luzon: 1944

WEAKLY we made our way along the road, guarded on either side by slouching soldiers. Twice Jamison, just in front of us, fell exhausted to the ground. With brute force the Japs shoved us aside and began clubbing him with their rifle butts and kicking his bare ribs. He groaned and the air rushed from his lungs in a piteous whine, but he struggled to his feet and stumbled on.

At our side walked old Colonel Esmond, naked except for an overseas cap he had found floating in the water. His tall, bony frame was like a skeleton covered with wrinkled, yellow, rubber skin. But he was helping a younger man, just a kid, who leaned heavily against the old man, weeping and groaning with every step. Then I noticed the gaping wound a bullet had torn across the young man's thigh.

All along men were helping each other as we came to the outskirts of a Filipino *barrio*. I had never seen Olongapoo. It was a pretty little village on the side of the green mountain. We cut around it and within a few minutes we came to a tennis court. I had never thought of a tennis court as being a prison compound before, but I could see that it would make an ideal one. It was surrounded by ball wire, rather like small chicken wire. Just a single cement court. Not too far to the side, just beyond the trees, were the former marine barracks.

They herded us inside the tennis court, pushing us back farther and farther until soon it was filled and more men were coming. I could see that there were easily eleven or possibly twelve hundred men. I knew that we would be awfully crowded here and the men were very weak.

There was just room for us to sit down. We squatted down with our knees in the back of the man in front of us. Then the rumour was passed about the group that the Japs were going to give us water. Water! Oh, God!

The unrelenting sun was hard and hot on my naked body. I could feel my skin blistering, and the skin of my friends was red in the tropical glare. Well, surely they would keep us here only a little while. Then they would move us to a place which would be more comfortable. Maybe we would be sent back to Manila. It would be embarrassing to be paraded back through the streets of Manila again, since so many of us had no clothes on. Surely they would send clothes to us before we went back to Manila. When I looked about, it was easy to see who had swum to land with all their clothes on.

Captain Dixon, who I knew could not swim and whom Rass had helped to shore, was fully dressed, even including an old blue denim jacket. Suddenly I envied and almost hated the fools who could not swim and had loaded themselves with all they owned and some of the gear the others had left behind. These men, whom we had used precious strength to tug ashore, now huddled, clutching their extra clothing, glancing with furtive eyes for fear a stronger man would tear it from them.

But we continued to wait and nothing was brought to us. The men were groaning and pleading for water. Many of us were desperately in need of medical care as well. But even men whose arms were dangling at their sides, broken and crushed, seemed to hold on, hoping that things would be better soon.

Things would get better and we would be all right.

We stayed there the rest of the afternoon and still nothing was brought in. Well, maybe in the evening. Maybe they're waiting until the sun goes down to take us out, for fear of American planes again. But as the evening rolled around and the sun was nearly gone and nothing had been done, we began to squat down, trying to make ourselves comfortable, knowing that perhaps we would have to spend the night there.

Abruptly a group of guards appeared at the gate at the end of the little tennis court and asked for five men. It wasn't long until they were back again and on their shoulders they were carrying five-gallon oil cans. My heart leaped. Oh, how I hoped that it was water!

They carried the water in and the prisoners began to fight among themselves. Finally an older officer begged one of the Jap guards to come inside. He could help control them and protect the water so that it could be divided fairly among the men.

By wedging us back until we could scarcely move they made room in the centre so that the water could be dispensed. One of the prisoners had a mess kit spoon, and after much debate and cursing it was decided that we would make an encircling ring of the men. As we passed, each man was given five spoonfuls of water. He held his head back so that he would not lose one drop, and then one of the officers dropped in five spoonfuls. The men cried that it wasn't enough, that there was more water than that. It was a thankless job.

I was very weak. I held my head back and felt the cool water dripping down inside my raw throat. I had never tasted anything so good. I didn't know that water had a taste. Water was surely the elixir of the gods.

It must have been 'way past midnight by the time the last of the water was given out, for the moon had risen high into the sky. 'Moon, palm trees, tropical islands,' I grunted. 'Nuts!'

I tried to sleep, but it was more like losing consciousness. I squatted with my knees huddled up against my chest, cramped and tired and weak. In the night I heard Hughes and Rass whimper in their sleep.

As the first rays of the morning appeared, the Nips brought in a garden hose and ran it through the fence and up the hillside and we had water, all the water we could drink. Men let it roll over them, gulped it down. It was a great sensation. Water, water, wonderful water.

By noon the prisoners had all the water they could drink. Their thoughts turned to food and medicine. But the planes returned and they circled over our heads as we looked up at the sky, afraid. They circled over us without harm, but we could hear them bombing the town and strafing. They would come right overhead and tip their wings. They knew who we were. As I watched them in the sky I heard Rass speak.

'If we can live through this period until they get us back
to Manila, they'll never get us to Japan. Just think of that,
all of you. Just keep your minds on it. We'll be free!'

How we wanted to be free, to be home again. To be
well again. To be free men.

The sun was blazing and the cement beneath us felt like
sitting on a hot plate. We were blistered and the water that
we had drunk was steamed out of our bodies. We were
weak from hunger and tired. Surely they would get us out.

When the sun went down I knew it was hopeless, for still
no food was brought. As it grew dark I felt a slight mist
in the air and the clouds were coming up. It began to rain.
It was cold, and we huddled together all through the night
as the soft misty rain fell. When morning came and the
sun reddened the sky above us, I could not but wonder,
'What would this day bring?'

It was the same as the day before. All day long we sat
in the sun, waiting, hoping, praying. Occasionally a man
died, and his body would then be pulled up to the front and
laid beside the fence. Each hour there seemed to be more
and more bodies there. But still many of the terribly
wounded held on against all odds, knowing that if they
could make this, they could make it through to the end.
Soon the Americans would be here. Soon we would be free.

In the afternoon, when we were all sick from the sun, Mr
Wata, the little interpreter, appeared at the gate. He had a
pile of white paper in his hand and he called to one of the
officers and handed it to him. It was a list of all the Americans who had sailed from Manila. He wanted someone to
call out and check the names of those who were dead, so
he would know who were not with us.

We made room while the officer who had dispensed the water walked to the centre. We pulled over the old referee's platform from where it stood at the edge of the tennis court. Our officer climbed up on it and began to call out the names. It was a long and tedious task. A name would be called and there would be no answer.

'Well, does anybody know what happened to him?' pleaded the officer.

Half the men were not listening, trying in their makeshift way to better their positions and worrying only about the sun that beat down on their brains and naked bodies.

'Well, does anybody know what happened to him?' he repeated.

'I think he passed out last night,' someone yelled. 'I knew him but I think he's dead. I think I saw him with the dead on the deck 'way down under the. . . .'

As soon as there was a definite assertion it gave birth to contradictions.

'The hell you did. He was in the back section near me and a bomb fragment got him.'

'How could a bomb fragment have got him when I saw him swimming away from the ship?' From someone else.

But still no answer to the name. Sometimes the missing man would speak up weakly because someone had shaken him and brought him to. Or the questioning went on for some minutes longer, establishing something, or establishing nothing. What had happened? Who had died?

For hours and hours the reading of the names went on and on. Occasionally a name struck our ear, the name of a friend, and we listened for the answer. When there was silence, we had a feeling that the man was better off. He was free. He was not sitting here with his body scorched by the sun.

When the sun went down the concrete suddenly lost its heat. The men who had been putting their hands on their burning shoulders were now shaken by chills and began to hug themselves. An effort was made by some of the officers to organize the men so they would be more comfortable. They tried to make rows of fifty men, so that they could intertwine their legs. They then would change their positions every so often.

But the wind grew cold at night and we were thirsty and hungry. Frequently men had to get to their feet and struggle to the side so that they might urinate. Diarrhoea was bloating the men and making them weaker. When morning came it brought a few warming minutes that were neither chill night nor hot day. There began again the tedious task of calling the roll, a rite which went on for hours and hours. I wondered what was the use of it. About six more men had died during the night and more men were dying.

Gradually the place became crowded with dead bodies. We tried standing the dead up against the fence. They began to smell and rot in the sun. Our third day in the tennis court we begged the Japs for permission to carry the dead outside. They allowed us to do so, and the bodies were taken out and laid on the side of the hill. The third day passed like the others, and the fourth day too.

We were now so weak and dizzy from hunger and starvation that none of us thought we could make it much longer.

Hughes was seldom rational, but stared with sun-reddened

eyes toward the green hills, muttering about games he had played as a boy in England. Weldon cared for him as though for a child. Once when they were asleep, Rass stared at them for a time and then turned to me.

'Did you know that Weldon was a twin?' he said simply.

'No, Rass, I didn't.' Weldon had never told me much about anyone except his mother. Odd, Rass' bringing it up in that flat, analytical way.

'He told John about his brother once,' Rass went on. He pressed the palms of his hands against his eyes. I knew he had had a terrible headache all day.

'Seems that Weldon's brother was weaker and smaller, kinda sickly. Weldon always looked after him and took care of him.' Rass slumped down with his head on his chest, preparing to doze off. 'Just thought you'd like to know,' he said sleepily and yawned. 'Caring for a weaker guy has done as much for Weldon as it has for Hughes. Necessary for both, I guess.' Soon I could tell by his breathing that Rass was asleep.

The evening of the fourth day, two Japs carried in a large sack of uncooked rice. It was given to one of the senior officers, Colonel Esmond, of our group. Again we formed our little circle entwining within itself through the tennis court. It took until late into the night, but each man received one spoonful of dry uncooked rice. He held it close to his chest, guarding it.

I put one grain in my mouth, chewing it gingerly and letting it bring the saliva into my mouth. It tasted so good and as it dissolved I put another grain in my mouth. I spent the night eating my little handful of rice. The next day it was the same. Each evening they brought us one sack of uncooked rice. The days went on and on, until nine days had passed. Nine whole days!

Now we were terribly weak. We looked at our skin and saw it hanging limp around the structure of our bones. There was no medicine, and nothing for the wounded. Gangrene had set in, and the putrid odour of rotting flesh was a horrible thing.

The last afternoon Rass and I held Kelly, a former member of the Fourth Marines. I sat on his arm with Rass on his legs while one of the American doctors with us cut his gangrenous arm away, hacking away at the bone with a borrowed Jap bayonet. I could hear it crunching. The boy just looked at the sky. He did not cry or yell. He just gritted his teeth.

'It's got to be done and I can stand it,' he said between clenched teeth. 'Soon we'll be free and that's all I'm looking forward to.' Great beads of sweat stood on his forehead, but his skin felt oddly cold.

When his arm was cut away we propped him up. We tried to get the Japs to let us make a fire. They wouldn't do it, but finally one of them handed in a piece of burning wood and the flesh was cauterized with the flame. The burning skin gave off a pungent odour but still the boy did not cry out.

The next morning the Japs came and said that all who could not walk would be executed. Every man would have to get on his feet and walk up the hillside about a kilometre to where we would be loaded on trucks. I struggled to my feet. I knew I could walk, and I felt sure now that we were going back to Manila. There we would have hot food again and medicine. Tenderly Weldon and Rass lifted Hughes to his feet.

As we started out I looked behind me. Lying on the tennis court were men who could not walk. The Japs began kicking and clubbing them. As I went through the gate I looked back again. Father Cummings made the sign of the cross above them while the guards lifted their rifle butts high over their heads and brought them crashing down into the skulls of the Americans left lying on the cement. The sickly thud of those beatings followed me, but I set my eyes on the hillside.

We struggled up the hill and were loaded on trucks. There were planes in the sky, but they merely circled and were gone. We started up over the mountain, circling along a narrow little pass, and gradually started down again. All through the day we bumped along the hot dusty roads until we reached San Fernando, Pampanga. We were unloaded and led through the streets into an old theatre building. But there was water, all the water we could drink, and we drank and we drank.

That evening two prisoners were taken out and when they returned they carried steaming rice piled high upon two corrugated iron sheets. It was our first warm meal of rice and there was enough for nearly two handfuls for each man. The rice was good, and we could feel strength and hope returning to us. It was hot and filling and it brought back life to our beady, shrunken stomachs.

We slept on the floor that night in the old theatre, with more comfort and more hope and more food in our stomachs than we had had in many days. I felt sure now of being able to make it. We would all make it.

About three o'clock in the afternoon of the next day we were routed out of the Pampanga Theatre and marched down to the railroad station. As we stood there waiting in the rail yards I looked at an aged locomotive with multiple bullet holes in it, which testified to what the American planes were doing. Slowly we were packed into box cars of the narrow-gauge railway type. They were thin little cars and they had been used to haul rice. Consequently they were nearly airtight when shut. We were loaded nearly a hundred men to each car, until within a few minutes the men were again suffocating. The train pulled out of the station and across the country. I turned to one of the two guards standing on either side of the doorway of the boxcar.

'Non judeski haitai san?' I asked one of them. I asked the time and I asked the day. The answer was what I had feared. This was Christmas Eve.

'Damn it! Quit thinking so much, Sid,' Weldon said in his gruff voice. 'That's what hurts you most. You think too much. Try not to feel. Try not to think. After all, you can't help it if it's the day before Christmas. Pretend it's the day before the Fourth of July. Don't let it worry you.'

I looked at Rass and I knew that he felt as I did, but he was trying hard to forget. As the train moved along I felt myself getting dizzy and weak. I was blacking out, but I jerked my head and gritted my teeth and tried to overcome it. The train went on. Day passed and night came. The train worked its way northward.

We were not going back to Manila, and every man knew it now. It was nearly midnight when we passed through a little town. I saw inside the doorway of an old Spanish church and heard the sounds of the midnight mass and the gentle singing of the Christmas carols. The Filipinos were celebrating Christmas.

The night dragged on. As the train wound its way through the mountainous district, I thought of a plan. The train kept passing little ravines that dropped away below us. These ravines were coming up with some regularity. I turned to Rass.

'Look. I tell you what we could do.' My voice was urgent but low, for fear the guards or the other prisoners might hear me. 'You and I will make our way to the doorway. We will ask permission from the Japs to take a look, and you will stand over at one side, and I will stand at the far side. I can see up front when the next ravine is coming. When I give the signal, you hit yours and I will haul off and slug mine. Then jump, and start rolling as you jump. The guards on top of the train won't be able to see us and they won't be able to shoot at us because we will be down in the ravine. We can get away. We'll get to some Filipino home and they'll hide us. They'll hide us because they know the Americans are coming. They'll be kind to us with the Americans so close.'

Rass smiled as though I was a prattling child.

'Do you think that you have the strength to run a hundred yards, let alone try to run a mile?' he whispered.

Then I realized how weak I was.

'I think I could make it. Don't you think you could try, Rass?' I was pleading now. 'Please! Let's try to make it away.'

He reached out and laid his hand on my arm.

'We'll stick it out, Sid. We'll make it. Don't worry. Just stick with me, and trust yourself, and trust God. We'll make it.'

I wanted badly to escape. But I couldn't go without him. I couldn't think of going without him. He had saved my life many times. Our friendship meant too much to me. I couldn't desert him now. Maybe he would need me again. And I knew I'd surely need him.

11 Christmas 1944

IT WAS very late at night, almost morning when the little train pulled into a station and we were ordered out of the cars. Wearily we unloaded and piled out on the open railroad yard. It was dark and stars still filled the skies. It was a beautiful night but rather chilly, as so few of us had clothes.

Father Cummings told me that the little town where we had stopped was at the northern tip of the island of Luzon, called San Fernanda del Union. Mr Wata, the Japanese interpreter, came and told us that we could lie down and rest. They would not move us again until daylight. We stretched out upon the open yard in the gravel and coal soot and waited for the sunrise.

I slept with complete exhaustion and had to be awakened in the morning by the tip of the Jap guard's boots and his grunting above me. It was early morning and the sun had drawn its red fingers of dawn across the sky. The Jap guards were yelling and we were herded across and up the street of the little town.

With sympathy written on their faces, people were peering at us behind their windows. We trudged along, helping each other, tired and hungry and weak, coming at last to what looked like an old convent school yard, deserted and empty. It had a high stone wall around it with broken glass embedded on top. We were herded inside the yard and told we would stay there until they let us out again.

The rest at the railroad yard had helped the men. Hughes, his fair skin black-streaked with soot, kept pulling on his long nose and encouraging the broad-framed Weldon in his wild dreams of hope. Rass' dark eyes were dreamy, as though he saw things I could not see. Once I caught him staring at Father Cummings while the priest prayed for a dying man.

'Soon it will all be over,' he muttered to himself more than to me. The discouragement in his voice let me know he was speaking more of life than of our imprisonment. Could I have known all that was to come, as I think sometimes he did, I doubt whether I could have faced it.

Inside the school yard was a garden with hibiscus bushes, bright with red and salmon-coloured blossoms. There were tiger lilies, grass and other bushes with green waxy leaves. Within a few minutes the men, in their extreme hunger, were eating the leaves of the plants.

Rass was eating some of the hibiscus blossoms and I tried one. I ate some of the leaves and they tasted good and sweet. In a short while, as though human locusts had descended on the place, there was not a leaf on any of the bushes. There were no flowers and men were eating the bark and even the grass along the paths. Over against one of the far walls I could see some lilies growing. There were some men there, but not very many. Rather than draw attention, I walked over slowly. I thought maybe I could get to them before they were noticed by the majority. White-faced men were sitting around them and they were

sick and vomiting on the ground. I walked over and grabbed
one of the lily plants and began pulling it up to get at the
bulb.

'Hey, fellow, don't eat those!' One of the sick men cautioned me. 'They're poison. I don't know what they got in
them but they'll make you sick. See what's happening to us.'

But I was awfully hungry, and I knew that some men
didn't have very strong stomachs. I went ahead and pulled
up the bulb.

It was a beautiful bulb and I cleaned it off with my hands
and bit into it. It tasted good, like a raw sweet potato. I
tore at it ravenously and gulped it down. In a few seconds
it was like an explosion in the pit of my stomach and I began
to vomit and retch. All of it came up, but I had a dizzy
sickness.

Soon a friend of mine came by and we all cautioned
him not to eat the bulbs. He made the same rationalization
as I, and he ate one. Then Rass came over. I begged him
not to eat any. He laughed at us.

'Ah, you guys are all just a bunch of sissies,' he said.

He too was sick. Pretty soon Colonel Esmond came over.

'Please, Colonel, don't eat them,' we cautioned. 'They're
not good. They're poisonous.'

'I can eat them. Hell, you guys are just sissies.' He had
a very pitiful sound in his voice. 'Hell, I'll live longer than
any of you. I know I can eat them. They won't make me
sick.'

He grabbed a bulb. I begged him not to eat it.

There was almost a sob in his answer. 'I've got to. I'm
so hungry.'

He too was sick. There must have been sixty to a hundred

men sitting around, all sick at their stomachs from having eaten the lily bulbs.

We stayed in the deserted school yard all that day. Later, toward evening, Rass and Hughes and Weldon and myself were sitting on the ground, not talking, trying not to think too hard. Then it dawned on me with a shock.

'Why, this is Christmas. This is Christmas Day and it's nearly gone.' I felt rather silly, and I turned to Rass. 'Well, Merry Christmas, Rass.'

He grew red in the face and angry.

'Shut up, you damned fool,' he said. 'Nobody but a damned fool would talk like that. You don't have to remind us of those things. Keep your trap shut.'

There was anger in his voice and in the looks of Weldon and Hughes. I should have kept my mouth shut. It was easier if no one put it into words.

As evening came on and the sun was sinking Mr Wata, the ugly little hunchback interpreter, came inside the compound again and told us that we would soon be leaving.

We struggled to our feet. Those that could helped the weaker and the wounded. We started out through the gates and down the road just as it was getting dark. We walked, it seemed for hours, until we came to the beach.

The sand felt good under our bare feet. It was still warm and we lay down on the beach and covered ourselves with sand, for the night was growing cold. I slept, listening to the caressing swish of the waves.

When the sun came up the next morning, I saw a large ship just at the breakwater. Barges were going out to it and returning with horses. Late in the afternoon the ship was completely unloaded. Then they told us that we must be prepared to leave.

We marched down to the piers that ran out into the water. They began to load us onto barges. We were carrying many of the men who were no longer able to walk, and we loaded them into the barges beside us.

Riding on the barges, with the launch chugging up ahead, my friends were all silent. Weldon never looked back. He kept his eyes straight toward the large ship, his white lips pressed in a thin line and his tight jaw set with determination. *Oh, dear God, don't let me think.* Now it was certain we would never get back to Manila, that the Japs would try to get us off the island even if we all died. I tried desperately not to think or feel.

It took until late that night to be loaded into the ship. They put us down into the hold where the horses had been. There was manure all over, and big horse flies which covered our bodies and began to bite. When we could no longer stand we lay in horse manure. But at least there was more room on this ship, because so many men had died. Already I could hear the huge engines in the depth of the hold starting up, as though they were impatient to be off before the American planes came over again. There were other ships in the convoy. It seemed a short time afterward that I heard the anchor coming up, and the ship started out toward the sea.

None of us talked because of the flies. We tried covering our eyes with our hands. If you opened your mouth the flies were so thick that they were in your mouth and over your tongue and you were spitting them out. The smell of

our filthy bodies began to draw more flies, until they were
crawling all over us. Rass and Hughes and Weldon and I
huddled together. Finally I slipped into a fit of deep, helpless sleep which gave neither rest nor relaxation.

When morning came some of the men had died. We
moved them out toward the centre of the hold, away from
the rest of us. It was nearly noon because the sunlight was
coming directly into the hold, when the Nip guards lowered
buckets of water for us. They threw tin cans down so that
each man would have a cup to drink with. A group took it
upon themselves to distribute the water. Each of us received
about a half a can of water.

The four of us took our water back to our little section of
the hold and sat down, not wanting to drink it right away,
torturing ourselves with the thought of how delicious it
would be. How good it would taste. I picked up my can
and let a small swallow of water trickle across my tongue.
With a shock I realized it was salty and bitter. It was half
ocean water. Our disappointment was so great that Hughes
began a hysterical weeping. Rass reached over and shook
him and Weldon slapped him across the face.

'Hold on, fella, take it easy,' Weldon said, with more ten-
derness than his slap.

We debated among ourselves. Could we drink it? Wouldn't
ocean water make us more thirsty than we already were?
But it was only half ocean water, I argued.

I looked around and in the little group next to us I
noticed all of the Catholic priests sitting together. My eye
met Father Cummings' and I smiled. He crawled over beside me and, putting one hand over his mouth to keep away

the flies, he said, 'Men, there is an old story about how these islands were populated. It is said that the Malays in their hollowed-out canoes travelled from island to island. They had no water to drink but ocean water. They had trained themselves from childhood to drink ocean water. It's been known in other cases that men have been able to drink ocean water and live. You could, I think, do it, if you tried, if you wanted and had faith. You could do it.'

Looking at the man, I felt that as long as I had my eyes on him I could have faith to do anything. He was very thin and less strong than the rest of us, with a skinny naked little body and scanty white hair. He was old enough to be my father. I thought of all he had done for me, and his long hours of just being beside me and helping me to keep faith.

'Father, stay close by us,' I begged him. 'The other priests do not need you. We need you here beside us. Stay with us.'

He smiled. It seemed that all he wanted was to have someone need him. He reached over and gripped my hand. I knew he was happy because we needed him. I lifted my can and drank the water. Though it was bitter and tasted bad, somehow it was refreshing. And then Weldon, never taking his eyes from Father Cummings, lifted his can and he drank it. And then Rass. And then Hughes.

It was that way each day. Once a day they would hand down big wooden buckets on ropes, filled with rice. Each man would crawl forward and get his share of the rice that would keep him alive. We crawled back and ate it together, and Father Cummings talked to us about a school of little children he had taught in Manila before the war, ragged little street urchins of Manila. Now he hoped, if God granted him the right to live, to be a missionary in Japan after the war.

'But Father, don'tcha think the bastards are hopeless?' Weldon grunted.

Father Cummings laughed. 'No, son, no one is hopeless.'

The days went by and I counted them. We were in the hold of the ship about five days. On the fourth day I heard that there were submarines below us. Suddenly I heard a roar as the ship sent a depth charge down into the water. The ship shuddered and I could feel the shaking jar of the explosion far beneath us. And here we are below the waterline, I thought. If one of the American submarines hit us with a torpedo it would come crashing through the guts of the ship and we would drown. The thought struck all of us at the same time. With a terrific RRRuummff! the second depth charge went off into the water and exploded below us.

Chills moved up my spine and I fastened my eyes on the face of Father Cummings. He smiled. He showed no fear. I knew that as long as he was beside me I could control my fear.

The torpedo did not come and after a while we were dully calm again. Days passed and I slept fitfully through them with exhaustion and hunger. We were always thirsty. I had torturing dreams of lying down in a cool mountain stream and feeling the water rush over me. Cool, cold, delicious water, running over my whole body.

Every day they lowered down our tiny supply of water. Once a day they lowered down buckets of rice. But the containers were not allowed to stay down. They had to be emptied immediately and sent back up for more rice because they didn't have enough to send it all down at once. They upturned the buckets on the floor among the manure and the filth. It was picked up by handfuls and distributed to each man. There were no toilets and the men, when they defecated, had to use the place where they were. Most of the men were having diarrhoea owing to the filth. They were bloated and passing blood. The flies covered us and I wondered how much longer we could exist in the filth.

All at once I heard some of the prisoners laughing. Then a few began to sing. Oh, the irrepressible humor that is part of the breath of life. They were singing a song about *benjou*, the Japanese word for defecate. They were singing to the tune of the famous Sunday school song of our childhood, 'Brighten the Corner Where You are.' They sang:

'If you have to benjou
'And the benjou is too far—
'Why, benjou in the corner
'Where you are. . . .'

12 January 1945

OFTEN I looked up above and saw the toothy, hunchbacked Wata glaring with distorted eyes through his thick-lensed glasses. Standing at the open hatchway, he grinned down at us. When the rice was passed around I saw what he considered funny.

A colonel who had once commanded an entire regiment stood, his eyes glazed with hopelessness, clutching his little handful of rice against his naked chest and eating it with filthy fingers. He was trying desperately to keep the flies away from it and to put the grains into his mouth without getting flies at the same time.

There were scientists with us, scholars, rich men. Misery had made us all alike. We were no longer men, save in brief flashes. Merely hulks of human flesh which contained only a desire to eat and a desire for water and and a hope and a prayer to live.

More men were dying every hour. We moved them forward and stacked them just beneath the hatch so that when Wata, or any of the other Japs, looked down into the hold he could see the yellow, emaciated dead. The Japs knew that this would happen to all of us unless we received more food.

One of the hardest things to bear, as each man was carried forward and added to the growing pile, was the look on Father Cummings' face.

'If only I could do something,' he would say. 'If I could give them the last rites, or be with every man as he died. Maybe he would hold on to his faith that last flickering moment before he departed. I don't care whether they're Protestant or Catholic. If I could just hold their hands and pray with them as they died. But there are so many. I can't be with them all.'

I looked around. Here were four of us, three of different Protestant churches, and one who didn't care what church but still believed in God. Not one of us was Catholic, and yet we all felt close to Father Bill. Because we knew he possessed that one thing that would save us all—if anything could.

One morning a dying man near us called out to Father Cummings:

'Father, please, I am afraid.' His voice came in a dry, rasping sound. 'Please, pray for me.'

Father Bill crawled over and knelt beside the man. The prayer came to me in a humming whisper I could not hear. But when he had finished, the panic-stricken man clutched the priest's arm with his long bony fingers. In the faint light I could see his flesh grow white under the desperate grasp of that hand. I thought maybe the man was crazy and started to move toward them in case Father Cummings needed help. But the wide pleading eyes held me back.

'Father, I've never been baptized.' Tears rolled across his shrunken yellow face. 'Please baptize me. I don't want to die without being baptized.'

'But, son, I have no water.' Father Cummings spoke as though to a frightened child. But I could see, as I knew he could, that the man would not live until the next ration of water was lowered into the hold. Father Cummings reached down and unlocked the man's grasp on his arm.

'I'll be back in a moment,' he said.

'Don't leave me, Father.' He was sobbing now.

Father Cummings crawled back to where we were waiting. But the look on our faces told him without asking. We had no water. Desperately he looked at the other men, but they merely shook their heads sadly. My mouth was dry like cotton and my throat cried for moisture, but I would gladly have given him water had I had any. Only one man kept his eyes averted suspiciously. In this struggle for survival I knew Father Cummings would not ask for what a man did not offer of his own accord. Finally he turned and crawled back to the dying men and knelt beside him.

I saw him run his tongue across his dry lips. Then he spat on two of his fingers and ran them over the man's forehead.

'I baptize thee in the Name of the Father, and of the Son, and of the Holy Ghost.'

Then he took the man's hand and held it while peace returned to the frightened eyes.

The stench of the bodies in the hold became so great that it was spreading to the upper part of the ship. Finally the guards threw ropes down into the hold and commanded us to tie the bodies together. They called some of the men on deck and allowed the bodies to be hauled up. Then the bodies were splashed into the water with weights to pull them to the bottom of the sea.

Each day, as the ship moved farther north, it grew colder, and we could feel the chill seeping down into the hold. We huddled together, trying to keep each other warm with our bodies.

One afternoon, when I was helping to drag another body and stack it with the rest of the pile, I stopped and looked up. Above me, standing on the deck and looking down, was a Jap private with a gun in his hand. There was a quiet look on his face, an expression almost of sorrow. He shook his head.

'*Keena doko, nehimo*,' he said gravely, and then in faltering English, for fear I had not understood him, 'I am sorry. I wish I could help you.'

I spoke to him in Japanese and asked him what day it was.

He looked back over his shoulder as though afraid someone would hear him.

'It's the third of January, 1945,' he said quickly. 'We're sailing into Takaow, Taiwan.'

I knew Takaow was on the southern tip of Formosa.

'We're sailing into the harbour now,' he said. 'It's a big harbour. Maybe they'll take you off here. I don't know.' He turned and walked away. I walked back to my small group of friends and told them the news.

'One of the guards just told me that we're pulling into Takaow on the southern tip of Formosa.'

It seemed to cheer them that we were in Formosa. We had been told that there were prison camps there and that conditions weren't too bad. Maybe they would take us ashore.

We were getting ready to tie up somewhere, because I could feel the anchor running out. The boat stopped its engines and settled down. We sat there for the rest of the day hoping. Two days passed. On the evening of the third day I heard planes circling in the air above the ship, and the spitting of anti-aircraft.

'My God! Not American planes here too.' I thought. I walked over to one of the Navy men with us.

'Do you think there'd be American planes here?' I asked.

'Why not?' he countered. Then almost regretfully, 'But I guess they aren't Navy planes. They're most likely coming from China. Army stuff.'

I walked back to my group and carried the news. I knew that we couldn't stand another bombing. Surely they would get us out. I couldn't understand why we were just sitting here in the hold of the ship. We sat through the night worrying.

Would they get us off before American planes could strike?

It was early the next morning, while the Japs were lowering the water into the hold, that they suddenly dropped the ropes and began screaming. We knew something was happening. All of a sudden I heard the planes diving in the air above us and the ship began shaking with the quick rattle of the anti-aircraft guns.

Quickly I grasped Rass' hand. Then I turned and looked at Father Cummings. There was a thunderous crashing above us. My stomach rushed to my throat as if I were falling through space. The ship leaped and bucked. Again there was the screaming roar of the diving planes. Like a trapped animal, I cowered against the floor.

'Oh, God, here they come again!' Hughes cried.

Then my brain was bursting. My eyes felt a blinding flash.

Bombs crashed down upon us. I heard a shattering, pulpy sound and warm liquid drenched me. A volcanic flash split my eyes again. A thousand hammers pounded against my body, dashing my head against the steel floor. Pungent smoke burned my throat. Things were falling like rain around us. I lost consciousness. Then I was jerked back by a chain of explosions bursting at the back of my brain. Something slashed like a white-hot knife down my spine, ripping and crushing my legs and hips.

My head cleared, but there was a horrible pain in my back. Smoke was thick and burning. Flashes of fire were everywhere. It was an inferno, with a din and rattle of guns above. A cave-like blackness engulfed me and I lost consciousness again.

When I came to, the roar of the planes was dim and distant. I had a sense of extreme, excruciating pain in my back and then suddenly I realized the fighting was over. A heavy beam was lying across my hips and a piece of a hatch cover on my legs. The floor was covered with blood and there were pieces of arms and legs and a head lying beside me, the head of someone I did not recognize. I looked around for my friends. Weldon and Hughes also had beams lying across their legs. White smoke floated in the air and burned my lungs like fire. My head was throbbing and my ears rang, dulling the pitiful cries of the torn and bleeding men.

I knew my legs were crushed. I was afraid to touch them, afraid to run my hands down for fear that maybe they weren't even there at all. There was no feeling in them.

I got up my nerve and ran my hand underneath the beam on my hips. The bones seemed to move at the base of my hips and I knew they were broken and my legs crushed. There was no feeling in them. They were numb.

Now men were standing up and walking around dazed. Some men were walking with their arms blown off. It seemed that there were only a few alive.

'Sid! Sid! Are you all right?' I heard Rass call frantically.

'No, I think my legs are broken,' I called back. 'Maybe my back.'

Then he was beside me. There was a bloody slash that ran across his cheek, but he was not seriously hurt. He walked over and looked down at Weldon and Hughes.

'I think they're both gone,' he said. 'They're both out.'

Then he bent over Father Cummings. Rass began to massage his arms and his face. After a moment or two Father Cummings sat up and he was all right. He wasn't hurt. He had just been knocked out by one of the beams. He and Rass came over and lifted the steel girder that had fallen across part of me and then the broken hatch cover.

'Do you think you can stand?' Father Cummings asked me.

I reached down and pinched my legs and there was no feeling. I seemed paralysed from the waist down, but there wasn't much pain. I looked up and I could see the look of concern on Rass' face. Father Cummings was looking at the mess around us, at the many bodies and the wounded men, and tears were in his eyes. He and Rass started to walk away.

'Don't leave me!' I pleaded. Rass turned around.

'Take it easy,' he said. 'We're just gonna try to get Hughes and Weldon out from under this mess.'

Father Cummings bent close to feel Hughes' pulse.

'Well, he's still alive,' he sighed.

Rass was bent over Weldon, massaging his arms and slapping his face.

'Weldon's alive too,' he announced.

I watched them open their eyes. They shook their heads dazedly. Rass was busy examining Hughes' legs. He hesitated a long moment before he told us.

'They're both broken and crushed.'

Father Cummings and Rass knelt beside Weldon and I saw Father Cummings shake his head.

'Well, he had only one leg broken, but it's a bad break,' he said. 'Part of the bone is protruding through the flesh.'

Rass came back over and knelt down beside me. He ran his hand across my forehead and through my hair.

'Stew, try not to be scared and afraid,' he said gently. 'We're going to try and help some of the other guys. Don't get frightened. We'll be back. Just hold on to your nerve.'

I watched him and Father Cummings walk around among the men, helping some to their feet, lifting beams off the others, and moving out some of the dead. Rass took charge of the section. He got hold of one of the American doctors, and they began calling for all the men who had any clothing at all to take it off and rip it up for bandages. They took pieces of the wood that had blown into the hold and used them for splints.

I began to fear that the planes would come back again. I knew I was crying. I couldn't help crying. I didn't want to believe in God. I wanted only to live. If the planes came back and struck again, none of us would live.

'Hey, Stew! Hang on to yourself, fellow.' It was Weldon's voice and I felt ashamed, because I knew his leg was broken

and yet he was holding on. I lay there, forcing a calmness
of spirit. Gradually, by pulling myself along with my arms,
I worked myself over and lay there beside Weldon.

'I'm sorry,' I said.

'Aw, forget it, Bud. I know how you feel.'

Then he started talking softly to Hughes, about home,
about his mother. I just lay there thinking about home. If
I never made it, I hoped they'd know how I died.

As soon as he could, Rass brought the doctor over to look
at us. I couldn't understand why there was no feeling in my
legs and no pain. The doctor was naked, and where was
his stethoscope? This is a fantastic dream, I thought hazily.

The doctor didn't say a word. He stood up and then he
examined Hughes and Weldon. Finally he turned to Father
Cummings.

'All three of them have broken legs,' he said, 'but this
boy,' and he pointed to me, 'I think his back is broken. I
don't think there is much I can do for them. I don't have
anything.' There was an almost apologetic tone in his voice.
I couldn't help feeling afraid and I looked at Rass.

'Do you think the planes will come back?'

'How could I know?' he said wearily. Then his face went
calm. 'Just don't think about it. If they come, well, after all,
you've made it this far.'

Father Cummings knelt down beside me.

'You've made it this far, boys, all three of you. Now try
and listen to me. Just keep your thoughts on the fact that
if you have faith, you can make it even now. You mustn't
let it whip you. You can make it.'

I looked to see if he was sincere. I knew that he felt I
could make it. I became determined.

The planes did not come back and all morning and late into the afternoon Rass and Father Cummings worked with the other wounded. Toward the middle of the afternoon the cries of pain, the weeping and the pleas for water were making a madhouse of the hold. Finally Rass and Father Cummings came back and sat down beside us. I could see from the look on Father Cummings' face how bad things were.

'How many are there killed?' I asked Rass.

He shook his head as though he didn't want to say. Then I asked him again.

'How many are there dead?'

'I counted two hundred and fifty dead,' he said. 'There might be three hundred, and nearly everybody's wounded, wounded badly. Many men are going to die if the Japs don't give us anything pretty soon.'

Then, very low, I heard Father Cummings praying. Praying to the God he believed in and that he wanted us to have faith in. I wanted to pray, but I couldn't. As the day stretched on I found myself at times crying for water, like the other men.

'Shut up, Stew!' Rass said. 'You're just wasting your energy and making yourself weaker. These other fools, if they would realize that and conserve their energy, they'd be better off. Crying for water isn't going to get you any.'

The day passed and then night came and the next day, until three days were gone. We lay there, and no water was given us, and no food. By now the stench of the blood and the rotting bodies around us seemed more than I could bear. Finally, in the middle of the third afternoon, I saw Colonel Olsen, who had been in charge of our whole group of prisoners in Davao, standing in the middle of the hold staring up through the hatch.

Above him I saw Wata's diabolical eyes and face. I looked again at Colonel Olsen. He had had an arm blown away and there was a rag tied above the arm as a tourniquet. He stared at Wata a while before he spoke.

'I ask nothing for myself,' he said. 'But these men are dying. In the name of humanity, in the name of the gods that you believe in, can't you do something for them? They will die if you don't give them bandages and medicine and food and water.'

Wata just stared, and finally his lips curled, showing his yellow teeth.

'They were your planes that bombed,' he said in his crooked English. 'They were your planes. We don't care if you die. They were your planes and they have killed our men too.'

He turned and left. I heard an almost hysterical weeping. Some of our officers were giving up hope. Then I heard Father Cummings.

'Listen to me, men! You must listen to me.'

The crying stopped and there was no more groaning. Then in his deep, clear resonant voice he began to pray. It was the Lord's Prayer. It floated like a benediction through the hold, caressing every one of us.

'Our Father Who art in Heaven, hallowed be Thy name. Thy kingdom come. Thy will be done on earth as it is in Heaven. . . .'

I felt that God listened, that God watched us and that God cared. The day passed into night and I slept until morning. When morning came I was more rested and felt better, but when I reached down and pinched my legs there was still no feeling in them. Weldon and Hughes seemed better too.

As though in answer to our prayers, the Japs lowered small bottles of iodine and mercurochrome into the hold and a few small rolls of pitifully inadequate bandages. Then they lowered buckets of water and that was more than an answer to a prayer. Rass brought the ration of water for Weldon and Hughes and myself.

We huddled together there, the four of us, making a ritual of it, drinking our little bit of water, and helping each other build anew his desire to fight. But I couldn't get used to the strange fact that there was no feeling in the lower part of my body.

'Does your leg hurt very much?' I asked Weldon. 'Does it pain you very much?'

'Aw, not much, just a little bit when I move.' He grinned and turned to Hughes.

'How about you, kid? How do you feel?'

Hughes smiled. 'They hurt some, not very much, but they hurt some. They're mainly kinda numb, but they hurt too.'

I looked around the hold at the men who were standing. I watched them walking about in their dazed, shell-shocked way, moving among the bodies. They were beginning to reorganize, however, to do what little they could to pile the dead in the middle of the hold. The stench of the rotting bodies was almost unbearable. The next day Wata said that those who were strong enough would have to move the bodies. They were going to take them out of the hold.

Slings were lowered slowly down and the dead were

stacked on the little rafts that were held by the ropes. They stacked the corpses in groups of about twenty-five. I watched the emaciated yellow bodies being pulled out of the hold, and I watched the tremendous effort on the part of the men who were moving them. These men, the living, were almost as much a part of the dead as the bodies. None of them had eaten a decent meal in many months now. They went about their work in a dazed, helpless way, lifting the bodies of their best friends, moving and separating the wounded from those who were dead. Finally, when all had been pulled up and lowered over the side of the ship to barges, Wata told five men to come out, and then he called down and asked five more and five more, until fifteen of the strongest men had left the hold.

They were gone many hours. When they returned late in the evening they told us what they had done. They had taken the bodies ashore and stacked them on piles of wood, where they were burned. It must have made a tremendous fire, about four hundred bodies burning. None of the men who had been out wanted to talk. They sat around dazed, as though they had seen something of which they and all of us would soon be a part.

Our life in the hold did not change. We were down in the hold nearly two weeks and men died every day and were loaded up and carried out of the ship. Finally Mr Wata again appeared at the hatch above us and yelled down that we would be moved to another ship. They were going to move us on to Japan. Then he ordered all who could walk to come up on the deck of the ship.

Weldon, Hughes and I lay there watching all of our

friends move away from us. We watched them climbing
up the ladders and out of the hold, and we could not help
wondering what would happen to us. Would they take us
with them? Or would they leave us, kill us, as they had
often done with the wounded who were unable to take care
of themselves?

Within a few minutes I heard the booms of the ship
moving. Then I saw the slings being lowered down into
the holds. Tied to the ropes were little raft-like affairs. With
relief I saw that prisoners were riding on them. When they
reached the floor of the hold they walked over and began
picking up the wounded and laying them on the rafts.

'Hoist away!' they yelled when the raft was full.

Rass and Father Cummings came down. They moved
toward us and Father Cummings went to one of the priests
who was badly wounded and helped lift him over and laid
him on the little raft. Then he and Rass picked me up very
carefully, one on either side of me, and carried me over
and laid me beside him. They did the same with Weldon and
Hughes. When the raft was loaded I heard them yell:

'Hoist away!'

We were pulled up out of the hold into the sunlight. The
boom went higher into the air and it swung out over the
water and lowered again. We were unloaded on barges,
while other barges were pulling away already loaded. There
were pitifully few men left now, as compared to the vast
number of us who had left Manila.

The launch began churning the water and chugging across
the bay, pulling us toward the next boat. There were many
sunken hulks of blasted ships protruding from the water.

When I looked at the large boat ahead, I felt a cold breeze blowing across the water. This would be our third ship.

I dreaded this boat with all the cold darkness of uncertainty, not knowing then that in it hundreds were yet to die.

13 Formosa to Japan: January—February 1945

THE NEW ship was smaller than any of the ships that we had been on before. But looking at the group around me, I could see that it didn't matter, because there weren't many of us left now.

I was placed on the deck of the ship and laid near the other wounded who were unable to walk. Already about fifteen of the men had died. Presently Father Cummings and Rass came over and knelt beside us.

Rass said to the three of us, 'Now you guys, hold on and don't worry. Father Bill and I will stick by you. You won't have to worry because you can't get around. We'll make it till we get to Japan. Just depend on us.'

I knew that if anybody could help me to make it, Rass would. I noticed that Weldon reached over and patted Hughes' arm. Hughes smiled for the first time in many hours.

When it came time to go down into the hold, Rass lifted me up in a fireman's carry on his back. He fell to his knees, he was so weak. Slowly, by grabbing one of the ropes, he pulled himself to his feet, then struggled down the ladder with me.

The hold of this ship was not as deep as the others had

been. We were very close to the upper deck of the ship and
the badly wounded were laid just beneath the hatch opening. Soon Rass and Father Cummings carried Weldon and
Hughes down and laid them beside me. We shivered together there in the hold, staring at the grey winter sky.

'Well, dammit, I guess it ought to be cold,' Weldon said.
'Here it is January the fifteenth, and it gets cold in this part
of the country. If they don't give us some clothes pretty
soon we'll freeze to death before we even get to Japan.'

It was late in the afternoon before the boat pulled out.
I knew if this ship didn't make it within a few days many
of us would not live. It was bitterly cold. There was still
no water to drink. One of the Japs told Rass that the water
tank on board the ship had broken and that they were
hauling all of their water. Consequently they would be able
to give us only a very little.

As the boat headed out toward the China Sea the Japs
lowered buckets of rice down into the hold and took men
on deck to help them. American prisoners were allowed to
work on deck. They carried slop buckets up and down for
us to urinate in and use for bowel movements.

Each day passed in about the same way. We were given
a small handful of rice to eat and about four and sometimes
five spoonfuls of water per man. Many of the wounded were
delirious or demented. Their screams before they died tortured us all. Men were becoming selfish now because they
had so little energy to give. The dying died unaided, without
help or solace.

In the evening, as it grew dark in the hold, Father Cummings stood and prayed. He started with the Lord's Prayer,
and then said a prayer for the day, and for those who had

died, and those who were dying around us. It grew colder
and colder, and some snow and sleet began to fall down in
the open hatch. We felt ourselves freezing. Our teeth chattered all the time. We were emaciated, almost bloodless,
and the cold was unbearable.

Finally we begged the Japs to allow the hatch to be
covered and laid over with canvas. They agreed. It made
a gloomy, yellowish, almost a ghoulish light. More men
died each day.

Some of the dying imagined they were home, back in
their childhood. Some talked as though they were playing
with their children, chatting with their wives, hearing an
old friend tell a joke. They laughed and chuckled. It was
a mad noise. I think hell must be very like that.

Rass and Father Cummings worked harder with us every
day. I could see their strength waning. But Rass moved me
and propped me up, and sometimes sat with his back against
mine so that I could sit up straighter. He did the same
with Weldon and Hughes.

I held on to each day, losing consciousness ever so often,
but gripping myself, afraid that if I relaxed, I might die. I
didn't want to die. I begged my friends around me not to
relax, but to hold on. They, too, would make it.

The men who went up on deck said that we seemed to
be sailing among little barren Chinese islands. Occasionally
the ship had to stop, go back and tow some ship whose
rudder or steering gear had broken. Precious time was
passing and more men were dying.

The wind was bitter cold now and sleet and snow were
falling into the hold again. The demented wandered around,
trying to catch the snowflakes that fell through the tiny

opening, and licking the floor where they fell. At last the men became too weak to carry up the *benjou* buckets of slop, which spilled over on the floor. The hold became filthier and filthier. We began to be crawled over by tiny things we couldn't see in the dark, which bit and stung us.

Finally Rass, who had gone up on deck to empty one of the buckets, told me that in the light he saw that they were lice, little grey lice. They were in my hair and in my eyebrows. If I closed my eyes to sleep they crawled over my eyelids and all over me, biting. It was strange. After all I had heard about other wars, only now were we meeting lice.

I watched Weldon and Hughes getting weaker. One day the Japs failed to give us water. They said the water was getting low because the trip was taking much longer than they had expected. They would be able to give us a little water only every other day. Yet somehow, my strength returned. Though I could not walk, I grew stronger even than Rass or Father Cummings. I began to pull myself about the hold, trying to help Weldon and Hughes as best I could. Rass and Father Cummings were so weak that they fainted with exhaustion. I tried to take over and care for Weldon and Hughes. Infection had started in their legs and they were burning up with fever. Their cries and mutterings, begging for water, were tortured, animal whimperings.

The Jap guards came down into the hold and stood at the edge of the ladder. They asked if there were any prisoners who had gold wedding bands, or West Point rings, which they would like to trade for water. Few of us had these things, but occasionally a man parted with his wedding ring for a rusty tomato can full of water. Sometimes before he could drink it, men would go crazy and fight him. He had to protect with his life the water he had traded for.

Each evening sanity returned to the men when Father Cummings began to pray. By now, almost all the other priests had died.

'There were eighteen, no, nineteen of us when we left Manila,' he recalled one evening. 'Now. . .' He didn't finish.

Each night the solace and the comfort that we received from the prayers was more than anything that anyone else could do for us. He gave us strength and hope. One evening, as it was getting dark down in the hold, Father Cummings stood and said his prayer. We tried to bed ourselves down so that we could sleep. Rass lay down close beside me.

'I'm afraid that Weldon and Hughes won't make it another day,' he whispered. 'They've been out of their heads now, delirious, for the whole day. They're weak and their temperature is high.' He sighed with resignation. 'Hughes is burning up with fever and his lips are parched and dry. I'm afraid he can't make it any longer.'

Rass fell back exhausted, almost unconscious. I could see in the dim light that Father Cummings was already asleep. In the shadows of the night a faint reflection of light was cast through the small opening into the hold. I reached over and touched Hughes' hand. It was very hot, and he was whimpering. Occasionally he cried out, 'Oh, God, give me water. Give me water.'

I reached across him for Weldon's hand and he too was crying, and then choking as he coughed. I ran my hand over his forehead and it was very hot. I had to do something. I had to get them water. If they had water it would bring their temperature down. It would save them. I had to do something for them.

What could I do? I began to crawl around, pulling myself by my arms. I dragged my helpless, foolish legs that had no movement in them, that were insensible to feeling, insensible even to pain. I pulled my body with my arms over to where many of the dead bodies had been stacked, hoping against all hope that maybe one of the dead had a ring on his hand that I could trade for water. But it was foolish. All of them were cold now, stone-cold and stiff. None of them had anything. If they had had any clothing at all, it had been stripped by the living.

I crawled back and lay down again beside Hughes. His whimpering went on. I had to do something.

I started pulling myself around among the wounded. I saw a man lying there. I couldn't see who he was in the faint light, but on his finger I saw the yellow gleam of metal. I reached over and touched him. He lay there groaning. I laid my ear close to his mouth. He was unconscious but groaning. I thought, oh, maybe he will die and I can have the ring. I waited and it seemed like hours, but still the man didn't die. The night was getting late. I wondered if I dared kill him. My friends needed the water.

He was going to die anyway. They needed the water now if they were to live. Weldon's face and Hughes' face and their tortured cries came to my mind. I must kill this man. I looked down and examined the ring on his swollen hand.

It was a West Point ring and I knew the Japs would give me water for that. I laid his hand down again and pulled myself up near his head. I started to close my fingers about his throat. It would take only a little pressure and the man would choke to death. It would be easy.

But I couldn't do it. Each time I touched his neck I heard the prayers of Father Cummings. I tried again, but I could not bring my hands to do it.

Suddenly I heard a shuddering gasp from the man. Then he no longer breathed. He no longer groaned. I laid my head down on his chest and listened. His heart was still. The man was dead.

Quickly I reached for his left hand and began to tug at the ring. But his hand was too swollen and bloated, and the ring wouldn't come off. I laid my head down on his chest and pulled the hand up where I could get better leverage. Frantic now, I tried hard. But it wouldn't come. I was desperate. I looked around for help. But I knew if someone else saw me, someone stronger, he would take the ring himself.

At last a plan came to me. I lay my head on his chest and, taking the hand, I began to use my teeth. I felt like a carrion ghoul, but I had to do it. Weldon and Hughes were my friends. If only I could get the ring, I could trade it for a cup of water and it would save their lives.

After a while the ring-finger came free. Slowly I worked the ring off the bloody stump. It came free in my hand. I did not know how long it had taken me to bite through the man's finger, but as I looked up I saw the light was becoming brighter in the hold. It was very early in the morning. As I looked around I saw the men still sleeping exhaustedly.

I pulled my body over, clutching the ring in my hand, beside Hughes and Weldon. They were still alive, whimpering, crying for water. I left them, and pulled myself forward to the front of the hold, near the bottom of the ladder. The sentry was standing above with his gun in his hand. I called up to him and raised my hand, waving the ring between two fingers.

'*Kempi, kempi. Haitai san. Mazu,*' I said in Japanese. 'Water, water, please.'

He stepped over and climbed down the ladder until he could see. He knelt beside me and picked up the ring in his hand. He examined it slowly, and then he looked down at me and handed the ring back.

'I bring water,' he grunted.

He crawled back up the ladder and I waited, looking around furtively for fear someone would see, someone stronger. After an eternity the Jap appeared at the hatch and climbed down. He held an old rusty tomato can. He handed it to me and it was full of water. I wanted badly to taste it, just a taste. I handed the Jap the ring and he climbed back out of the hold.

I looked around carefully for fear someone would see me. Then I used my arms to pull myself, slowly inching my way back to where my friends were. The light of morning was coming down into the hold and the men were beginning to stir. Some were sitting up.

I tried to crawl faster, faster, for fear someone would see the water can. At long last I reached Weldon and Hughes and crawled up between them. I wondered whom to give the water to first and I felt Weldon's head. It was terribly hot. I set the can on the floor beside me and pulled myself around behind him, edging my shoulder under his back to lift him up. Gradually I propped him to a half-sitting position.

'Weldon! Listen to me,' I said. 'I'm going to give you water.'

'Oh, water!' he cried out. 'Please give me water.'

I laid his head against my shoulder and held it there. Then I reached with the other hand for the can and lifted it gradually to his lips.

'Slowly now. Take it easy, pal,' I said. 'Take it easy. You're going to get some water.'

As the water touched his parched lips he ran his tongue across them, tasting the cool liquid.

'Water!' he screamed, and thrashed his arms crazily, striking the can. It fell from my hands and rolled clattering across the floor, spilling the water.

Men yelled, 'Water!' Men scrambled all around me, throwing themselves on the floor, licking with their tongues the water that had spilled there in the filth. I watched them and I knew the water was gone. Weldon was whimpering and crying for water and the water was gone, all gone. I could get him no more.

Slowly I laid his head back on the floor of the hold. I felt that all was lost. There was nothing I could do now. I was exhausted. I did not care if I lived or died. There was nothing I could do.

I laid my head down on Weldon's chest and began to cry. I felt the sobs working through my lungs, shaking my whole body. I wept until I lost consciousness through sheer exhaustion.

2

When I came to, Father Cummings was shaking me by the shoulders.

'Wake up, lad. The water issue is coming down and you'll want your water. These boys—won't need theirs.'

I raised my head. Rass was holding Hughes in his arms.

In the ghastly yellow light I could see the tears forming and rolling down across his cheeks. He looked over at me and nodded his head. I knew they were both dead because Weldon's body felt cold under my hands.

I knew they were both dead. And I couldn't cry. No tears would come.

Slowly Father Cummings and Rass pulled the bodies over where the others were and laid them there. When the water was passed around I didn't want mine. I couldn't think of water now. I didn't want anything. I could only follow Father Cummings and Rass with my eyes. They begged me to drink the water.

'You must drink your water. You've got five spoonfuls today.'

I didn't want any. If only I had had the water last night maybe it would have saved their lives. Without thinking I said, 'Give my water to Hughes.'

Rass smiled and patted my hand. 'Water won't help them now. They need nothing in this world.'

'Take it easy, fella.' Father Bill laid his hand on my head. 'You're gonna be all right.'

From that time on I looked forward every hour for night to come, when Father Cummings stood and said his prayer again. I lived only for that prayer of faith and hope. It was the only strength I had. His voice was like the voice of God to me. I knew that Rass felt the same, Rass, who was always so much more religious than I. He was now so weak that it was all he could do to stand. Yet I knew he lived too for that prayer in the evening.

Men were dying at the rate of twenty and thirty a day. Every morning their bodies were wrapped with rope and drawn up through the hold and dropped into the sea. Each day I watched the bodies going up into the sky through the open hatch. The rope swung out across the deck and I heard the sound of the bodies as they splashed into the sea.

I missed Weldon and Hughes very much. Lying together helpless as we were, we had still kept up each other's spirits. We had talked of home. I had remembered that when I was a little boy and sick with the flu, lying there in my bed, my mother had brought a bowl of hot potato soup with little egg noodles floating on top. How good it was. I had told them of that and it had helped a little. Almost happily Hughes had remembered the hot beef tea that his mother used to make. Now, with both Rass and Father Cummings busy every waking moment, I had no one to talk to.

One afternoon Father Cummings crawled over to pray for a dying boy and did not come back. Rass went to look for him. He found him unconscious through exhaustion, so white and still that when he brought him back and laid him near me, I was frightened.

I knew I could not hold on without him. I was afraid to ask Rass if he was dead. Not saying a word, Rass shook his head.

'No.' He laid Father Cummings beside me. I sat up and began to rub his arms and his hands and his face. Rass helped, and soon life returned. His eyelids flickered slowly and he opened his kind grey eyes.

'I'll be all right, boys.' He smiled wanly.

But he wasn't able to walk any more. Rass cared for the two of us now. Father Cummings had been passing blood many days with dysentery. He was so weak that he could not walk. His lips were parched and cracked and his hands moved convulsively up and down his throat. I knew that he couldn't make it much longer. I prayed silently to myself that I would die before he did, that I would not have to see him die.

But that evening, as it was growing dark down in the hold, and the faint light that came through the hatch was nearly gone, he begged me, 'Can you lift your arm behind me? I can't stand, but my voice will carry. They will hear my prayer.'

I pushed my shoulder in behind him and put my arms around him and held him up. Faltering, he began to speak.

'Men! Men, can you hear my voice?'

Slowly he began to pray. 'Our Father Who art in Heaven, hallowed be Thy Name. . . .'

The cries of the men became still. I concentrated on the voice that soothed me and gave me strength and the will to live. Then I felt his body shiver and tremble in my arms. He gasped for air and there was a terrible pain written on his face. He gritted his teeth, sighed and went on.

'Thy will be done—on earth—as it is—in Heaven.'

I felt him tremble again as if he wanted to cough. His hands fluttered and his eyelids almost closed. Then with superhuman effort he spoke again.

'Give Us This Day. . . .'

I felt his body go tense all over. He relaxed and his hand fell by his side. I waited, but his eyes looked straight ahead. The eyelids no longer flickered. I knew he was dead, but I continued to hold him, afraid even to move. Rass crawled beside me. He lifted Father Cummings' hand and felt for his pulse.

'Lay him down, Sid,' he said evenly. 'He's gone. Lay him down. He's gone now.'

I cradled his head against my shoulder. I didn't want to lay him down. I couldn't bear to face the fact that he was gone.

'Go ahead, Sid. Lay him down. Lay him down, he's gone,' Rass said firmly.

I moved from behind him and laid his head gently on the floor. Then I noticed that the hold was quiet. The men had gone off into their exhausted, hungry sleep. Rass reached across the body and gripped my arm.

'Sid, he died like he would have wanted to die, praying to the God that he believed in, to the God that gave him strength.'

'Why did he have to die, Rass? Why did he have to leave us?'

'Don't think about the fact that he is gone. Try to think of his last words. The last thing he tried to give us.'

Rass went on calmly, 'You know his last words were, "Give us this day." We must try only to live until we can see the sun up in the morning, you and I, and we'll make it. Live only for one day, for just twenty-four more hours.'

Without answering him I laid my head back on the floor. I lay there with my eyes open, just thinking. An hour or so later I heard Rass speak again.

'Do you want me to move the body?'

'No, Rass. Leave it here until the morning. Keep him here with us until the sun comes up in the morning.'

All through the night I didn't sleep. I lay there with my eyes open, thinking of all the man had done for those he

felt suffered more than he because they did not have his
faith. He had tried to give it to them, this thing he called
faith.

When I saw the first ray of dawn coming down into the
hold I knew that we had lived for the new day. If God gave
us this day, we would make it until the next morning. We
could make it for one day and that was as far as we could
think ahead.

Rass picked up the body and carried it over and laid it
with the rest. The ropes were let down into the hold, the
booms cranked and the winches moved. They tightened the
ropes around the body. I could see Father Cummings' emaciated body with the ropes wrapped around it.

Slowly the body started to rise as though it was floating
out of the hold. When the sun struck Father Cummings'
body it seemed to reflect a golden light. I watched that
golden light and the body as it floated higher and higher
up into the air. I saw the light with the body move out
across the deck. Then I closed my ears against the sound
of the bodies as they went down into the water.

Rass and I tried only to live for one day, painting a picture
in our mind. If we lived again until the first rays of the
morning sun shone down into the hold, then we would be
in Japan. We would have food, we would have warm clothing, and we would have water. At night Rass lay down beside me, and sometimes he lay on top of me to keep my
body warm. He rubbed my senseless legs.

'You've gotta keep the circulation going because they're
gonna be all right. You're gonna walk sometime when this
is all over and you'll be glad.'

I was glad for his warmth, for although they were numb,

there was something cold, awfully cold about those legs. Rass worked desperately to keep us both alive. We went on each day playing the intense game for our lives, praying for one more day.

One evening I heard the ship pulling into a harbour. With a clamour of chains the anchor ran down from the ship.

'You'll be taken off,' one of the Japs yelled down into the hold. 'You'll be taken off tomorrow.'

'Rass, do you know what day it is?' I asked.

He thought a minute and then yelled to a friend of his across the hold. 'Do you know what day it is?'

'I think it's the last day of January or maybe the first day of February.'

We went through the night, concentrating and praying that we would see the sunlight, tense, afraid to relax, afraid that in our relaxation we would be released and never know the morning.

During the night I heard the ship manoeuvering in next to the pier, which bumped against the sides of the ship. As the early morning light began to show above us, the Japs appeared and ordered us all out on deck. Japs came down and helped to carry the bodies up. Other guards came down with litters and loaded those unable to walk. Rass stayed beside me, holding onto the litter while the Jap guards carried me. There were no Americans strong enough to carry the weak and the wounded.

When we were laid on deck I began to be afraid, knowing how they treated the wounded and the sick. I knew I must stay with Rass. I was afraid that because he could walk they would separate us. Horrified, the Japanese medical soldiers began to run among us, spraying us with disinfectant and holding their noses. I knew how we must smell after all our days down in the filthy holds.

The cold grey sky hung low as a blurry winter fog. From where I lay I could see the lava-coloured, rocky islands stretching away, barren and hopeless, dotted with stunted, leafless trees. Along the docks swarmed kimonoed women stevedores, their weather-reddened faces like apples pitted with cloves. On the opposite side of the boat ran dung-coloured water, yellow as sewage. The slum smells of the Oriental city mingled with coal soot from hundreds of smoke stacks were blown over us by an icy wind.

They ordered all that were able to walk ashore. I crawled off my litter and began to pull myself along. There were others with me, moving on their hands and knees. We crawled down the gangplank and out toward the pier. I could not stay with the wounded. I knew I had to stay with Rass. I had to stay with him even though he was too weak to help me any longer.

He straggled along, and I crawled, pulling my legs behind me, just using my arms. They herded us out across the pier and into the street. Snow and sleet were falling, and the ground was wet and slushy. Feebly I pulled myself, and my teeth began an uncontrollable chattering. My hands and arms were blue with the cold. I had never been so cold in all my life. The other men too were bitterly cold. Their bodies were blue and their lips purple. A man would drop into a coma by the road. We went nearly three blocks. The blocks were like a hundred miles.

Finally we crawled into an old, empty warehouse. The group of American prisoners left was pitifully small. Maybe

three hundred, maybe less, I could not be sure. Out of all
the thousands.

We huddled together in the middle of the cement floor of
the old warehouse, trying to keep each other warm with our
bodies. It was useless, for the winter wind sought us out
through the many open windows. But there was a water
faucet in the building and men were filling cans and bringing water to those who could not walk. Rass got water and
brought it to me.

'Hold it in your mouth,' he said. 'Hold it in your mouth
until it gets warm, because it's very, very cold. It's so cold
it will cause cramp if you drink it.'

I took a swig of water in my mouth. I wanted to swallow
it but it was terribly cold. I held it in my mouth until I felt
it growing warmer and then swallowed.

Soon the Jap guards came in carrying huge buckets of
hot steaming rice. How I wanted it! They passed among
us, ladling it out in little cardboard containers. Nothing had
tasted so good and so warm in all my life.

'See, we're gonna make it now,' Rass smiled. 'Everything
is all right. Let's stick together and we'll be all right.'

I smiled, nodding with my mouth full of rice. At last we
were in Japan. I could not know that the biting wind was
blowing a cold, ominous note of death.

14 Modji, Japan: February—March 1945

THINGS ARE never as we hope them to be. After the rice was eaten we continued to huddled there on the frozen cement floor, the cold winds blowing in through the open doors and windows. The weather here was about the same as the State of Washington, I knew. The State of Washington in February.

Trying desperately to keep warm, we huddled there all the rest of the day and through the night.

Men froze to death and many of us had frozen arms and legs. Yet with every ounce of will I wanted to live. Once during the night I looked up to see a sentry standing there shivering in his heavy clothes. As he looked at our poor, starved, naked group I wondered what could be in his mind.

Then I felt sorry for him. I knew he could not help what he was or what he thought. Civilization had come hard to Japan. Most Westerners look upon the Japanese as the most progressive of the Orientals, with a civilization of many hundreds of years, but that is not so. Everything that the Japanese possesses, his national dress, his kimono, everything that he has is an adoption, most of it a poor imitation, of what he has seen. His writing is copied from the Chinese, his dress is adopted from the Chinese. Only ninety-odd years

ago, just before the Civil War in America, Japan first discovered Western civilization and those ideas we accept as
commonplace. The Japanese fought hard to assimilate Western ideas. But no nation can span centuries in decades. In
the twentieth century, when they set out to conquer America, their social system and their state ideas were still those
of the early sixteenth century.

I thought back to the history of England at the time of
King Henry VIII. It had not been unusual for a lord or lady,
displeased with a servant, to have him boiled in oil or pulled
apart on the rack. The horror of the galleys was known all
through Europe. The Japanese, I thought, have sixteenth-
century ideas of humanity and a twentieth-century objecti-
fication. We of the West have given them planes, cars, tanks
and guns. They have learned to fly these planes, to drive
these cars. But it will take generations to change their
thinking. They are used to beatings from their own kind,
from those who are of higher station and class. How can
they look upon us with compassion in their hearts?

This was a life no different than they would have expected were they in our hands. Looking at this lone sentry,
I knew now that our hopes for the mainland were wrong.

The thought tightened me inside. I looked at Rass and
I knew he had known for some time. Our life would be very
little different until the Americans came.

I closed my mind to it. I must not think that way or I
would not be here when the Americans came. I must make
myself believe that they would come tomorrow. Something
would happen tomorrow.

When morning came the Japanese walked among us, picking those who were most ill, the weak and the wounded.

They separated us from the rest. They divided the others into two groups. They loaded my group, the sick and wounded, on trucks.

'You are going to a hospital,' the Japanese guard said.

I wondered what kind of a hospital these people would supply. As the trucks bumped along the street, I asked Rass if he knew where we were.

'Yes, this is Modji, a city on the northern tip of Kyushu,' he answered. His voice was flat and listless as though he no longer cared about the future.

We reached an old building, a dilapidated wooden structure. We were carried in, those who were not able to walk, and we were put in two rooms. Along the tops of the rooms near the ceiling was an opening separated at intervals by pieces of two-by-four lumber. The opening was about six inches wide and ran all the way around the edges of the room. Other than that there was no light and no window.

The room was vacant and bare and the floor was damp and cold. They placed me on the floor. Looking around, I counted forty-nine men, including Rass and myself. That meant that there were probably fifty-one in the other room just opposite, for I knew there had been exactly a hundred when we left the warehouse.

A Navy Officer who had been in Japan before the war told me that this building was a typical hospital used by the Japanese to house their insane.

The doors were opened again and the Japanese sentries came in. Counting them out one by one, they gave each man a blanket. They brought in two buckets for voiding ourselves and set them in the centre of the floor. Gratefully we wrapped up in the blankets, rolling ourselves tight. Their warmth felt good to our bodies.

Then the Japs went away and in an hour they came back and set two buckets of water in the middle of the floor. They said this would be our water for the day. That evening late, they brought in a little bit of rice for each man.

We continued to live just so day after day. No medicine, no additional attention of any kind. Hope gradually receded from the hearts of the men around me. One by one, they began to die. Some days the Japanese neglected to bring us any food at all. Occasionally when we cried out, begging for food, they brought in buckets of their leavings, their slop, and dumped that in the middle of the floor. We crawled forward, eating from the floor with our hands.

The days dragged into weeks. More men died. Every morning the Japanese came into the room. If a prisoner was in a coma they caught him by the feet and pulled him across the floor and outdoors into the snow. In a few minutes he would be frozen. Then they stacked him with the other bodies waiting for burial.

It grew colder and the snow and the storms beat against the thin walls of the building. February passed and then March. Rass could no longer walk. He lay all day in a semi-coma. There were only four of us left alive in the room. One day I noticed Rass shivering. He was terribly cold. We contrived that if another man should die, we would steal his blanket. Maybe the Japanese wouldn't know it.

That evening, just as it was getting dark, I saw a large grey rat working its way gingerly toward us, sniffing. It worked its way around the buckets. Playfully it scampered

back and forth across the floor. I watched it. Suddenly I
knew that the rat would be food. I could eat that food. I
looked around, trying to find something to kill it with. Near
the corner of the room was a piece of wood like the broken
handle of a mop stick.

Slowly, trying to be as silent as I could, I moved my way
over and grabbed the piece of mop handle. Then I inched
myself toward the centre of the room and waited. I watched
the rat sniffing around the edges of the blanket. It worked
closer toward me. I watched until it was just a few feet
from me. I waited. Soon it was only a yard from me. Using
the last ounce of my strength, I threw the stick. The strike
was good and the rat bounded in the air, then fell over on
its back, kicking its legs convulsively.

I grabbed the rat, holding it tight, and pulled myself back
beside Rass. I jerked the rat's head off.

'Oh, Sid,' Rass pleaded. 'You're not going to eat it.'

I felt a little contemptuous of him, but I wanted him to
share it.

'Rass, you can eat it with me.'

'No!' He shook his head and turned his face away.

I devoured the rat, all of it except the skin, even chewing
on the bones. I knew it gave me strength. I felt better than
I had in many days. I lay down to sleep. Rass looked over
at me with hostile eyes. He almost hated me for eating the
rat, and I was ashamed. But what difference does it make, I
thought defensively, if only you live.

The strength did not last and with the days passing I
felt myself growing tense with fear that I might relax for
just a moment. Then I would die. I was even afraid to sleep.

I began to have a dream, a terrible dream. I dreamt I was in a coma and it was morning and that one of the Japanese sentries was dragging my body out of the room and into the snow. I tried calling to him, screaming and calling to him that I was not dead, that I was only in a coma. I screamed and screamed, but my voice made no sound. I woke up shivering all over, shaking from head to foot. Rass was gripping my hand.

'You were screaming, fella,' he would say. 'Just calm down. You're gonna be all right.'

The dream occurred each night. We were no longer talking to each other. We no longer gave each other encouragement. We seemed to know what the other was thinking about. Finally I felt that Rass might not want to live any more.

'Rass.'

'Yes, Sid,' he said calmly.

'You are holding on for each day, aren't you?'

He turned his back on me and said, 'Let's not talk about it. I don't want to talk about it'.

The next afternoon when the cold wind was pouring through the opening around the ceiling of the room and we could hear the wind beating against the building, Rass turned to me.

'Sid.'

'Yes.'

'You know, Sid, I don't believe there is a God.' His voice was even, utterly without emotion. 'I don't believe there is any God. All I know is that when I'm dead I'll never be tired again. I'll never be cold or hungry or beaten. I might not have rest or sleep. I won't even have anything, but that will be better than this. I don't even care if there isn't a God.'

'Rass, no!' I cried.

'I don't even believe there is a God.' He shook his head and closed his eyes.

I gripped his arm, shaking him. There was a faint flicker of his eyelids. But his sunken eyes no longer moved. They were quiet now. I knew—that he was dead. I grabbed him by the shoulders and began shaking him. I was crying hysterically.

'Oh, Rass, come back! Come back, Rass!'

But I knew it was no use. I could not bring him back so that he could change his last words. Dying, he denied the God he had believed in. I began to shake him again.

'Rass! Wake up! Come back, Rass! Don't give up!'

I laid my hand on his chest, crying. Then I began to pray.

'Oh, God, forgive him. He has suffered so. God, please forgive him. He didn't know what he said.'

I tried to make myself believe that Rass had not known what he said. But he was very rational. He had known what he was saying. I was afraid, cold and terribly afraid. 'God, please forgive him.'

I lay back on the floor, weeping. I lay there many hours and thought. All my thoughts were a prayer, and I counted over all the good things Rass had done, the way he had lived and his hopes, the way he had helped me and other men, the way he had cared for Father Cummings. I knew his faith had been as strong as mine. Then I began to wonder. Was he right? Had he discovered just before he died that there wasn't a God? I felt cold inside, and I was afraid that I was going to die. I gripped myself, holding every muscle tense.

'Oh no, God. I know You're there. I know You can see us.'

I lay there thinking back over all I had been taught by Father Cummings through the years, through the long, torturing, hungry years in prison camp. He had died and he had not blamed God. Then I remembered something he had said, many years ago it seemed now. When I questioned the acts of the Japanese and some actions of the Americans. I asked if God would punish them. He turned, laying his hand on my shoulder.

'Sometimes, son, men know not what they do. They cannot help sometimes when they lose faith in themselves, sometimes even in God. But God is just. Your God is a just God.'

Suddenly I felt stronger again. I reached over and touched Rass's body. It was growing cold now. I looked down at his face. It was strange to me that I had not noticed how very thin he had become, how sunken his cheeks were. He had suffered, he had wanted to live. He had been good, always kind and good. I looked up, closing my eyes, and I could feel God about me. I knew that God forgave him.

Christ's own words came to me like a whisper:

'My God, my God, why hast Thou forsaken me!'

All at once I knew that God had taken Rass home. God was good.

2

The terrible loneliness of the wind blowing against the fragile framework of the building and through the narrow opening along the ceiling was my only sound. But it was poor company, like the constant eerie cooing of many pigeons.

The room, which had seemed so small when we first came, now was infinitely large. Lying alone on the floor, counting every crevice and mark on its walls, I began to feel the personality of the room. The damp and musty floors gave forth a mouldy smell, like an old storm cellar. The two by-four rafters seemed to sag a little more each morning as I counted them.

Here is where I shall die. It was odd, but I was not afraid to die. For the first time in my life, I had no fears. I had always been afraid to die alone. What had I wanted? Someone to cry over me? No. To talk to someone about the feeling of watching it come.

Curious, the differences in light through the tiny openings in the walls. More often now there was a reflection of the sun sparkling in the light. It would not be long till spring. Spring, and the earth breaking again in freedom. I would never see the spring. I had cheated death too long. Seeing how long I could hold out, keeping myself tense, almost laughing with the morning light.

A dying man, they say, is supposed to see his whole life unfold before him. Why did those scenes never come? All I could think of was the men I had known through the long, hungry years of war imprisonment. They tramped through the past, not all good or all bad, but a human blend. Some weak, some strong, but never always weak or strong. My mind stopped along the way to watch a man drop by the road in the Death March. Saw again the boy Rass helped to die in the foxhole long ago. If I strained, I could hear Ohio's laughter.

Men I had never liked came to mind also, wearing deeper lines in their sad faces, all bearing the great indelible stamp of human dignity. Creation's goodness burned in all men. Most were led by the ram, some were eaten by selfishness, many were besieged by fears. Yet the flame was there, like a pilot light waiting for the right touch.

Someone told me once the world was cracking up. Look at the dangerous philosophies eating into our civilization today, he said. When I repeated this to Father Cummings he only smiled.

'Men said that during the French Revolution, so we must be cracking very slowly.'

Men would always respond like tuning forks to what was right and good, I thought. Great indeed was the human dignity of God's image.

It was growing increasingly harder to catch the morning light. Sometimes I felt myself drifting in currents that moved so swiftly that I could grab nothing to hold on to. Sometimes the light faded quickly and I knew I must have awakened late in the day. The Japs had brought food and water and were gone before I had seen them.

I tried to imagine what it would be like to go home again. Would streamers fly from the boat and people on the docks sing 'Auld Lang Syne' as they had when we sailed? Or would the war be over and unspoken like a dread, remembered nightmare?

I tried to remember the taste of decent food, but it would not come. I could only think of huge tubs of hot rice, and bending over them, feel the steam warm and damp against my face. It would be good to fill that horrible longing that never left me night or day.

Once I awoke and there was no light coming through the opening. I had missed the day, maybe two. I hoped I would not die like that. It would be better to meet it with the light, my eyes open, feeling the great numbness creeping through me.

In comas I imagined I was home again. I would run up and down the red gypsum hills of my childhood, feeling the dry Oklahoma wind brushing against my cheeks. Or I stood on the crest of a hill, looking away to the valley below me. The clay of my lost hills climbed brilliant red in a sun that followed a quick summer rain. The bright yellow-greenness of the tall grass glowed through the canyons and in the ice-blue sky I saw a white bird flying, gliding and circling in happy freedom.

Oh, to be free, to go home again. One morning I heard a sparrow's frantic chirping. Then it was gone, followed by the drumming patter of rain and the lonely constant wind whispering: *You can't go home again.* Then the loneliness was almost unbearable and I closed my eyes tight, trying to shut away the memories of home.

But they came anyway. The aroma of freshly ground coffee in a grocery store, people laughing, a cash register ringing. The smell of cedar and pine at Christmas time and children's sticky, wind-kissed faces. Burning autumn leaves and the crushed minty flavour of chrysanthemums, and schoolboys on bicycles, gliding along without touching the handlebars.

I would grab a leather strap to brace myself against the forward lurch of a streetcar, and hear the conductor's clamorous ringing of the tolls. And people all around, tired, weary, or happy, but always alive and free. Blue, red and yellow neon signs reflected crazily across black wet pavement and the hurried click of high heels blended with the rustling crackle of plastic raincoats.

My mother's face, smiling sadly at some long-forgotten childhood lie. The warmth of an extra blanket laid across me in the night, and the soft closing of a door. My father's blessing at the dinner table, never changing, intoned with the same inflection year after year. Finally I slept again with the wind moaning in my ears.

Once I opened my eyes and a sentry was bending over me. He shook his head sadly and walked across the room. At the door he turned and looked back, pointing with his finger to the can beside me.

'*Mezu,*' he grunted. '*Otsui.*'

I nodded and he went through the door. He had brought me hot water to drink and was a little embarrassed by his kindness.

The cold grey dampness depressed me now. I wondered why I could not relax. The light in the room grew watery and dim and I blinked my eyes. So terribly tired. So much easier to close my eyes and sleep. When I opened them again it was pitch dark. Far away I heard the groan of a fog horn or maybe a factory whistle.

In the darkness I tried to lie awake, but I could not. Drowsiness crept through me and my arms were numb and cold. Somehow I did not care so desperately to see the light of day come back again.

15 Through August 1945

'*I SAY, ARE* you English?'

A voice echoed above me like someone calling down a deep well. I fought myself through a space in time toward the sound of that voice.

'I say, can you hear me? Are you English?'

I opened my eyes and there was a face. My eyes focused. There were many men, white men. They stood around me, some of them kneeling beside me.

Are the Americans here? I wondered. Have they come at last? But as my eyes focused more clearly I saw that the men were dressed in prison clothes. No, the Americans had not come. I had been alone now in the room many weeks. I had felt the cold of winter receding. It had been so long since I had had someone to talk to that I found myself unable to speak. My tongue was thick and my throat seemed paralysed. A guttural grunting come from my throat.

'I'm afraid the poor bloke is just about done in,' I heard one say. 'I don't think he can talk.'

Behind him I saw a sentry standing. He grunted something in Japanese which I could not catch.

'Well, let's get him, let's pick him up,' the one in front said. 'You chaps help me get him on m'back.'

'Phew, he sure is dirty!'

They lifted me to the back of one of the largest men. Then they wrapped a blanket about me.

'Funny thing to me the bloke ain't dead. Looks to me like he'd be already froze.'

I listened to their conversation as they carried me through the door and out into the glittering sunshine. The snow was receding. There was a first breath of spring in the air. Then I seemed to lose all contact with the world. Once I awoke on a train. A man was holding my head up and feeding me something that tasted sweet and good. Then he spoke again in his English voice.

'It's a bit of Red Cross Klim, a little bit of milk. It'll be good for you. You've got to get something down you.' I swallowed and it tasted very good.

Then again I awoke, hours later, and someone was trying to put clothes on me. A man put my arms into a shirt sleeve, and a coat on me, and pulled trousers over my legs. Then they were gone again.

I awakened once more, lying on the grass in a little park. The sky was clear and blue through a T-shaped Shinto shrine. An ancient red-tiled pagoda, with an odd curved roof pointing toward heaven, stood not far away. There were many prisoners around me. Two of them walked over and knelt beside me.

'He's one of your men,' the Englishman said to the tall blond man beside him. 'He's an American all right.'

'Yeah, I wonder how the poor guy held on.' It was good to hear that American voice.

'Well,' the Englishman said, 'I don't know. Ever so often I think we're going to lose him. But then he comes back again, all right.'

'Where in the world did you find the guy?'

'Well, we were coming up over from South Modji, and we stopped at some little building and the Nips made us go in and get this guy. We don't know anything about him, but one of the Nips says he thinks he's an American.'

'Wonder where he could have come from,' the American said. 'Might be some guy that was shot down in a plane or something. Or he could be one of those guys that was on that shipwreck we heard about. It's hard telling.' Then he patted me on the shoulder. 'Anything I can do for you, fella?' he asked. 'Anything you want? Anything I can get for you?'

I tried to say something but it was an effort. Finally the words rolled out.

'No, no, nothing.'

'Well, bud,' he said smiling, 'just hang on and we'll see you through.'

Later one of the English boys fed me a little milk. Nothing had ever tasted better to me. It was sweet and good. Then I lay there for a while and I was alone. The men were standing in groups, waiting for something. I did not know what it was. Later one of the English boys walked over and sat down beside me.

'We're going to take a trip, you know,' he said. 'They're going to take us over to Korea. That's what we're waiting for.'

I nodded my head.

When I looked around I saw that spring had come to the islands, for there was a cherry tree, beautiful with its pink and white blossoms. Beside me in the grass was a violet, a little purple violet. It looked beautiful, clean, alive. Then things became hazy again. Once I awoke and we were on a boat. When I came to again I was being carried out into the sunlight and down a gangplank. I heard someone beside me talking.

'Whew! I'm glad that trip only took us five hours. Good thing it was a quick one. You can't tell what might have been in those waters.'

'This is Fusan,' I heard the American say.

I felt stronger. The milk they had been giving me was doing its work. I noticed a native Korean standing near in his long white flowing robes and high stovepipe hat, their national dress.

Later one of the Englishmen fed me good, hot rice. There were little pieces of fish in it and it tasted heavenly.

Time passed. I slept. I was fed. It was all hazily unreal. I still felt a certain tension, for fear that something good was happening and that I might lose it.

Finally I opened my eyes to look up at the clear blue sky and the sun shining. One of the men knelt beside me.

'How're you doing?' he asked.

I nodded my head. 'What day is it?' I asked.

He laughed. 'Why, it's the end of April, almost the first of May, lad.'

'Do you know where we are?'

'You're in Mukden, lad. This is Mukden, Manchuria. They say this is not a bad place to be. It's not in the rice country, you know. They grow beans and corn, and there's a lot of nourishment in those things. You're going to get well. You're going to get your strength back.'

He lifted me and I was loaded onto a truck. There were many men there and they were all very kind.

'I think the guy's a little chilly,' one of the men said. 'He doesn't have much blood.'

He took off his overcoat and laid it around me. I thought it was a very kind thing to do. They did not know me, and they were sharing with me what they had.

The truck approached a high wall. Gates were swung wide and the truck bumped over a narrow road inside the compound. The red brick buildings looked good and things were clean, like an American prison. There were many prisoners, healthier and stronger than any I had seen in a long time.

We were taken out of the trucks and carried into the buildings. They brought each one of us a bowl and soon a man came around with a large bucket. With a dipper he poured out a meal of thick bean soup. I tasted it and it was wonderful. I ate slowly, for it was more food than I had had in a long time.

'How are you doing, son?'

I looked up. The man had a stethoscope around his neck. An American doctor! The surprise on my face made him smile.

'This boy has had a pretty hard time,' a Japanese said in clipped English.

I looked behind me. There was a Japanese with a white coat on and he had a stethoscope around his neck. He bent over and felt my wrist.

'I'm going to leave a little box here by your side. They're vitamins. I want you to take them,' the American doctor said. 'I think you're going to snap out of it all right. I'm going to see to it that you get some milk. We've got some Red

Cross supplies here and you're going to get some milk every two hours.'

I lay back, content. Gradually my fear of relaxing went away. As the days flew by I grew stronger. Although I could not walk, I was healthier, and I was clean, and I was warm.

Summer came late in Manchuria, but it was a beautiful summer. The men laughed and joked. I could not let myself believe that freedom was coming. Yet they joked about it and were sure that it was near. They carried me out and laid me in the sun where I could feel the warmth surge through my body. Everything was good again in the world. Soon I would be going home. June wore away into July.

I began to plan the things I wanted to do when I went home. The promises I had made to the boys about seeing their parents. I thought of the things that home meant to me. The things that freedom, and being home, would mean. I thought of seeing women again, white women, and being again where people laughed, where laughter was good and life was good.

I wondered if ever again things would worry me. I thought what I would do with my life. I had never asked to live, but God had spared me. Now I knew there was an obligation within me to justify my life. I must do something.

My mind wandered back to the times when Rass and John and Weldon and Hughes sat together around the fire in the evenings. We talked about the things we wanted to do when we were free and we were home again. Rass had wanted to go into the diplomatic service. John had wanted to be a professor again.

'I'm going to be a writer,' I said. 'I'm going to write novels.'

We used to laugh about it. They were interested in the things I wanted to write about. Once, when we were very hungry, John had turned to me.

'Some day, Sid, I wish you'd put me in one of your books.'

'Yes, Stew,' Rass said. 'I wish you'd write a book about this, about all of us. Will you? Could you do that for us one day? Write a book about all of us. Something that we could keep.'

I remembered what I had promised them. I would write a book about them some day. But I felt cold inside and I thought, 'No, they'll never read that book now, that book I'm going to write about them. About their faith and hopes, their goodness and their beliefs.'

August was passing with its heat. I was feeling good and bathing myself in the sun. Suddenly I heard a tremendous commotion. Guns were going off in the city beyond the walls. There were many rumours. Some said there was a revolution going on.

That evening there was a terrific roar and a crashing sound. The huge wooden gates at the entrance of the compound crumbled. An engine groaned and a tank clambered across the fallen boards and rolled its way inside. Another tank followed through, and then another. Soon there were many tanks inside the compound.

Breathlessly we wondered what it all meant. The tank turrets opened and men clambered out. They lifted their helmets and I saw they were white men. There were smiles on their faces. I was afraid to hope. . . .

Prisoners rushed out to meet them. Soon they were cheering, yelling and laughing. One of the men rushed into the building.

'They are Russians! We are free! We are free at last!'

Smoke still floated peacefully over the old Manchurian city. I could see a small section of the ancient wall. I was afraid to look behind me at the wildly cheering men for fear they would not understand my feeling of unreality.

Freedom. I tried rolling the word silently over my tongue. This was just a dream. At any moment I would turn and hear Rass' voice or John's low muffled cough.

'Give us this day,' I mumbled aloud. Turning, I watched the happy men. Suddenly I was laughing too.

No one slept that night. Everyone laughed and talked till daylight. I heard hundreds of whispered plans, ambitions built through hungry years. When morning came we were told that as soon as the airstrip was repaired, American planes would come in and take us out.

That afternoon I heard many planes overhead. They took me to the window again and I looked up. The sky was full of falling parachutes of all colours, red and yellow and white. The looked beautiful floating toward the ground with odd shapes attached to them, not men. Then I heard cheers.

'They're boxes! Red Cross boxes! Food! The Americans are dropping food to us.'

It was a glorious celebration when the boxes hit the ground and were opened up. There were delicacies we had not dreamed still existed. Chocolate. Candy. Coffee. Meat, all kinds of meat. What a celebration feast we had. Men who had been unused to such things were sick, but they tried again, laughing because they were unable to retain the food that was so rich and good.

When the planes finally arrived, one of the American doctors came to me.

'We're sending the worst cases out first. You are going on the first plane.'

I was going home. When we were carried out and put on the trucks, the men cheered and clapped me on the back.

'You made it, boy. You made it!'

The truck pulled away from the compound toward the airfield. I was lifted into the plane on a stretcher with the other sick and wounded.

At last the plane took off, roaring down the runway, and I felt the release as the plane lifted from the ground. Slowly we gained altitude, circling lazily in the air, like the white birds gliding over the hills in my dreams. From my litter strapped to the wall I could see through the porthole.

The plane straightened out, moving south. Far below me was the Great Wall of China, like a ribbon running across the earth.

Soft white clouds moved beneath us. The sun shone a tinge of gold upon them.

We were happy, for we were going home.

We were the living and at last we were free.